JUST BECAUSE

YOU CAN

DOESN'T MEAN

YOU SHOULD

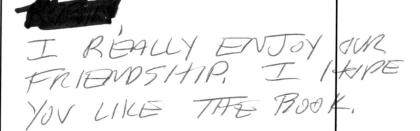

I REALLY ENJOY OUR
FRIENDSHIP. I HOPE
YOU LIKE THE BOOK.

JUST BECAUSE YOU CAN DOESN'T MEAN YOU SHOULD

Keys to a Successful Life

Mike S. McConnell

iUniverse, Inc.
New York Lincoln Shanghai

JUST BECAUSE YOU CAN DOESN'T MEAN YOU SHOULD
Keys to a Successful Life

iUniverse books may be ordered through booksellers or by contacting:

iUniverse
2021 Pine Lake Road, Suite 100
Lincoln, NE 68512
www.iuniverse.com
1-800-Authors (1-800-288-4677)

Because of the dynamic nature of the Internet, any Web addresses
or links contained in this book may have changed
since publication and may no longer be valid.

The views expressed in this work are solely those of the author and do not necessarily
reflect the views of the publisher, and the publisher hereby disclaims any responsibility
for them.

ISBN: 978-0-595-42851-9 (pbk)
ISBN: 978-0-595-87190-2 (ebk)

Printed in the United States of America

I dedicate this book to my darling children, Claire and Michael. My reading of *Who Moved My Cheese* during our family vacation at the Wilderness Trails Dude Ranch in the summer of 2001 inspired me to write it. I read the short book during the vacation and found it very insightful. I thought to myself, while I was reading it, that it was very valuable and that everyone should read it at a young age. That is when it hit me. With my collection of affirmations, my success at Enron and my desire to write, I should write down items that have been valuable to me and that have made us a strong family, which was financially secure and successful. If I had such a roadmap, it would have really helped me. I could also share it with my friends and play around with completing a book and publishing something. A small piece of advice from this book could make a huge impact on someone and might, just might, be the different between success and failure.

This is one man's story and I felt compelled to write it.

Claire and Michael,
Daddy loves you

Contents

Acknowledgements

This is very difficult. So many people have contributed to this work, and they continue to contribute, because it truly is a work in progress. Writers like Anthony Robbins, Denis Waitley, Og Mandino, Wayne Dyer and Dr. Norman Vincent Peale all had a profound effect on me. Each provided an element or an attitude that became a building block for the next. Each is part of the foundation that supports me. This foundation is complete only when I add my parents, various friends, teachers and, of course, my own immediate family.

As I acknowledge these profound thinkers and speakers, I must also recognize my friend, former partner and boss, Fritz Brinkman. Fritz introduced me to the power of affirmations in 1990. I believe I was meant to be his partner and to help him lead the company though a difficult time. In turn, Fritz was there for me and taught me that a man can do whatever he sets out to do, especially if he truly believes and has the proper state of mind. Our relationship certainly had its difficulties, but the experience changed me forever, for the better.

My list of affirmations is an accumulation of years of studying, watching and collecting. I cannot imagine how many hours I have spent reading them, writing them down and then adding them to my collection. I wish that I had kept a list of acknowledgements to give proper credit to each one. Very few are actually mine; most resulted from my captivation by someone else's thoughts and observations.

Ultimately, though, my primary and most significant influences were my parents, especially my dad. I am a younger version of him in many ways. My values, my business acumen, my work ethic are all his. Decisions I have made reflect what he taught me, especially my refusal to take short cuts, to let easy solutions tempt me, or to push an ethical situation. My goal was to grow up to be like him. I sure hope I have. It is hard to express the influence of the rest of my family as well. The impact of my wife Chris, my mom Judy, my sister Anne, my brother Mark, the kids and friends touched on every aspect of my life. I could write an entire book about the influence of each person. Thank goodness, family does not expect that, that they know in their hearts their importance in my life, and that each one's personal signature is a part of me.

I am who I am because of everyone above and so many others whom I did not have space to list, and I thank each one of you.

There is another as well. Erin Rice had a great deal of influence turning this from my fantasy into reality. I had a lot to say and she was able to turn it into something that said it so much better than I ever could have expressed myself. In fact, she not only made this book turn into a reality but also made it into something of which I can be very proud. She edited it all, gave me encouragement along the way and even made it seem that I had command of the English language.

Introduction

I wrote this book, quite simply, to help my children. It covers many topics, each one a segment on the journey to success; a journey I want my children to begin while they are young. Hidden within any one of these pages, in either text or affirmations, is an element that can lead to a successful life, if you are willing to embrace it. Everything I have written has played a part in my success in business, in life or in the plain fact of who I am.

Affirmations have been a huge influence in my life. In addition, I believe any one of them could change your life, too. If you think I am exaggerating their effect, well, you're wrong. One simple affirmation might influence a serious decision or change your life direction. Now, consider the events that result from that decision and the subsequent decisions and resulting events. The add-on effects are endless. So, if you read only the affirmations and not the text of this book, you will still come out ahead.

A word about the title I have chosen. It is significant. I watched a company that won "Most Innovative" in the country for five straight years move into bankruptcy, scandal and total chaos, literally overnight. Why? I believe the truth is that it was coming to an end for a long time. We just didn't see it. As I documented my own ideas about success, I recognized—in retrospect—the warning signs that had been all around us. They were important items like culture, values, the way many leaders or groups treated customers and employees; situations that should have been noticed and corrected. We did things because we could do them—not because we should do them. I think Enron crossed the line between "could" and "should" and never actually saw it. Moreover, it happened at many levels, from matters with the Board to our contention that "gray" financial structures were within the rules. These structures may have been within the rules, but I'm not sure that means we should have used them. If we had paused to contemplate "could" versus "should," I am convinced Enron would be a solid and growing company today.

I am also wrestling with a question as I write this book: I was successful at Enron, but why didn't I get in trouble or get accused of any wrong doing? Is it any one thing I did? Or was it a series of actions? I don't know, but this book is—in part—an attempt to figure that out, too. Being innocent of any wrongdoing is not enough and cannot be the only explanation. I know several people who went though terrible times being "accused" or "questioned" as if they were guilty of something—and I know they weren't guilty of anything.

One other driving reason for writing this book is to make sure I remember not only what Enron did wrong but also all the things they did right. The company and its people did many things incredibly well, regardless of what other people have written or assumed about almost everyone there. I learned so much during my tenure there. I think about the lessons learned in my continuing business decisions every day.

I hope this book will force contemplation with everyone who reads it. I hope that when you are bothered by or stuck in a situation, you will think about this book and want to see how I might have approached it. Did I succeed or not? Why? If you do this just one time and it helps, then I guess I will have done what I set out to do. I will certainly have made my point!

Enjoy and ponder. You might not agree—and you certainly don't have to. However, I do ask that you acknowledge that the contents of this book did work for someone: Me.

Section 1—Personal Philosophies

Chapter One:

Affirmations

What can I say about keeping and looking at affirmations? It has been a big part of my life for more than 10 years. I began in my days of working at Excel Resources with a man named Fritz Brinkman. He believed in affirmations and in the power and influence they have. He had a collection of his favorites and always started his day by looking over them and contemplating their meaning. That is when I picked up the habit. It has profoundly changed my life and thus our family's life. I do believe that being in the right state of mind allows you to look at things differently and makes you better and able to achieve a lot more.

In 1990, I made a decision that would change not only our lives but my attitude as well. I joined a company called Excel Resources. Fritz Brinkman was the founder and CEO. He was a self-made man and was a millionaire many times over. He did it not by formal education but by hard work and belief. He believed he could make it. He knew it. Actually, he was over the top on the entire concept. A maniac. He had the greatest collection of positive attitude and self help tapes probably anywhere in the country. He actually listened to them at night while he slept. He was a great believer that you are what you think and that it was very important to start the day off with the right attitude and approach to the day and/or problem. He looked at affirmations every day and believed they were vital to life. I modeled myself after his behavior so that I could be his partner and run his company the same way he would run it.

My collection of affirmations is well over 100 pages long. Amazing what can happen when you stick to something for a long time. That is a lesson in itself. In my collection of affirmations lies the secret of success and of living a balanced, happy and successful life. Whether I am reading, collecting or typing them, they all influence me and bring new ideas and thoughts into my brain. This is very powerful and I believe anyone can use affirmations to change his or her life.

I have been very blessed in my life. There are many, many reasons why but one very important reason deals with attitude. I attribute a great deal of my success in life and work toward my general attitude. We develop attitude over a lifetime of living and thinking. My parents have always approached life in a positive way; it is a way of life. Even in very hard times, they acted differently than most. They have tackled their fair share of adversity, survived and come out stronger then before. I have never been as proud of them as I was with the way they conquered cancer in the late 1990s. Mom stepped up and took care of Dad and Dad never missed a day of work during his radiation treatments. Twice.

People frequently ask me why I am so successful at such a young age. I believe the main reasons are that I respect others, I ask for help when needed, I share credit and I believe in myself and that I can accomplish anything. I mean anything. There is always a way, if you're committed. I do have doubts, sometimes often, but I have so many people who believe in me that I figure, "How can everyone be wrong?" I think it goes back again to attitude. I guess I really do believe that you can accomplish anything and that hard work, trusting your instincts and beginning the problem in the right way do make a huge difference. Scientific studies certainly back this up. The placebo effect is one, people's reactions to finding out they have cancer and the success rate of living is another. The mind is a very powerful place.

I began my collection of affirmations in 1990 and have continued it ever since. It is very addictive because there are so many wonderful and inspirational expressions and sayings out there just waiting for someone to read them, and heed them. This is my collection of affirmations, or life adjustments, and "state" management. Embedded in here is the answer to all problems in life. Look at these every day, or when you are ready or feel a need, and they can change your life. I think it is like going to church. When life is not going well, church sometimes draws you near and actually calls out to your soul. I think this is the same thing, and it echoes the belief that "When the student is ready, the teacher will come." Many, if not most of these expressions, sayings or stories have roots in religion and originate in the Bible.

I have pulled these sayings from a wide array of sources and people. I also carry a pocket index card for keeping track of ideas and obligations during the day and each one starts with a chosen expression on the top. This makes me ponder its meaning during the day. I can identify various authors and books by sections in this writing. As a start, it begins with numerous references by Anthony Robbins from *Unlimited Power*. He got it all started. *Unlimited Power* and the *Personal Power* program both had profound effects on me and on my family's life. My thanks will always go out to him. I will get a chance to thank him personally someday. I have had the opportunity and privilege to meet with two other "life coaches," Dr. Denis Waitley and Og Mandino. I could not actually thank them enough for how they affected future McConnells and me. Without a doubt, I would not have been as successful without those three men.

I keep my affirmations in chronological order, collected as I found them. I haven't ever taken one out or thrown one away after the fact. They were all included for a reason at the time I saw them. Many of these, actually all, are personal. Some will not make any sense to anyone else, but this is how I developed the collection.

As you read on in this collection, be clear of its power. I am absolutely convinced that we could find solutions to many of today's problems with people in the pages of this book. The answers are here, if you care to find them. In fact, nations have changed with single lines in this collection. If it could save a nation, it could change an attitude. This is a collection of greatness. A collection of life itself.

Enjoy and pass on to someone you care about. It might just make a significant difference in someone's life; certainly, it can take them in a new direction with a different approach to a problem.

At certain periods it becomes the dearest ambition of a man to keep a faithful record of his performances.
—Mark Twain

Better to write for yourself and have no public, than to write for the public and have no self.
—Cyril Connolly

Writing is the best way to talk without being interrupted
—Jules Renard

We are a species that needs to understand who we are. Sheep lice do not seem to share this longing, which is one reason they write so little.
—Anne Lamott

How do I know what I think until I see what I say?
—E.M Forster

I write entirely to find out what I'm thinking, what I'm looking at, what I see, and what it means. What I want and what I fear.
—Joan Didion

Quantity produces quality. If you write only a few things, you're doomed.
—Ray Bradbury

We do not write because we want to; we write because we have to
—Somerset Maugham

How vain it is to sit down to write if you have not stood up to live.
—Henry David Thoreau

Write down the thoughts of the moment. Those that come unsought for are commonly most valuable.
—Francis Bacon

If I don't write to empty my mind, I go mad.
—Lord Byron

Anyone who believes you can't change history has never tried to write his memoirs.
—David Ben Gurion

The reason one writes isn't the fact he wants to say something. He writes because he has something to say.
—F. Scott Fitzgerald

KEEP A JOURNAL

Without question, I have lived the most blessed of lives. Every day is wonderful, even if I forget it occasionally in the day-to-day grind and the living of life. The journey is not always easy, even in the best of times. A person's life is made up of events and actions that all have a cumulative effect on their future. Each action causes the next action. Each course, a new course. Although this is easy to understand intellectually, it certainly isn't as easy to live. I do believe that a person should live his or her life to the fullest and approach life everyday with growth, trying to improve his life or the life of his family. Little things mean everything.

In 1992, I began keeping a journal. An odd little event started this. I went to Specs restaurant in downtown Houston (it doesn't exist anymore) and visited its room of American presidents. I saw a picture of Chester A. Arthur. Although I am an avid student of history, I didn't remember who he was and it bothered me a lot. It made me think about all the things that I couldn't remember and that nagged at me. I took two steps that day. First, I started reading about the American presidents and started a personal history. Over the years, I ended up reading many, many books on the history of the presidency and all the men that held the office. I learned a lot about each man's leadership and actions how his actions affected America and its history. Each event changed the course of history. The changing course and corresponding new changes in course shaped a nation and everyone's lives in the country and world. I became an even bigger student of history. Years later, I still find myself in bookstores searching for new books on the American presidency. I still buy a couple each year.

The second step I took has to do with the fact that I have never had a good memory, and it bothers me. So, I decided to write a summary, actually an outline of all the events of our lives as the McConnell family unit. It began with my marriage to Chris in 1984. I still cannot understand how God found it in his heart to let me find and marry Chris. That is another story in itself. That outline put many things into perspective and was a good project and highlight of our lives. However, there was only one problem. It did act as great reminder of all of the events of our lives but it was extremely boring and dry. The *Life* project was a perfect outline for a book or story, however. I then used that outline as the basis of my journal. When I first started working on it, it was just for fun but it soon became my hobby. I thought that someday, my kids, my grand or great grand kids might really enjoy reading about Mom and Dad. We forget so much of life; the details and feelings seem to go away forever. All those feelings are hidden inside but they all play a part in who we are. With that said, it would be great to be able to go, years after the fact, and re-live or remember exactly what was going on in our minds during that time. Even going back a couple of years brought up events and emotions that I had simply forgotten or maybe simply put away in the back of my mind.

I am a big Star Trek fan, both the TV series and the movies; and in *Star Trek 5*, a character who could identify, feel and take away a person's deep-rooted pain was trying to find and lead the ship to God. He went up to Captain Kirk after helping all the key characters in the movie and offered to "take away his pain." Kirk refused and explained that his pain was part of him and made him the person he was. I think that is very true: Life experiences certainly make up the person. There are lessons in life; what happened and how you reacted to those situations and circumstances becomes part of who you are. This journal is just that. It is a summary not only of our lives but also of how we approached life.

The other significant thing my journal taught me was simply to put things in perspective. Events that were so important at the time, especially problems, simply were not significant in the big scheme of things. Actually, I had forgotten some very quickly. Things that were so big, so scary or seemed insurmountable were totally gone from my memory. When I re-read them I thought, "Oh, yeah." I had completely forgotten them. These events actually weren't so big and scary after all. I couldn't even remember them later. This realization has really affected our family and our approach to situations.

So many things happen for a reason and are linked with other events for a reason. My journal is a story of teamwork and partnership, of God and of trust and so much more. I will keep it up over my life; I must. It is an obligation as much as a project or hobby. In addition, you never know, maybe, just maybe, someone else may want to read about our family, to learn about who we are, just what kind of person I am and the kind of people we are as a family.

Anthony Robbins really started all of it for me. He stated in *Unlimited Power* that if your life is worth living, document it. Go ahead, start your journal. It will grow with time. You definitely don't need to do it daily, but take action. Start it. It is fine to drift away from it for long periods. You will come back from time to time and be glad that you had started it.

I have talked a lot about perspective. There are many times in life that you may feel are dark or desperate. The way to get through it is to think. Think about where you are in life. Sit back and really think or ponder. If you asked someone to make a documentary of your life, what would it say? What would it include? How much of your current situation would be part of the documentary? If you take an honest assessment, it probably isn't much. I won't belabor the point, but it is true. The opposite is also true. If it is a decision that might make the documentary, think long and hard about it. Write down the positives and negatives. Only time (or the documentary) will tell whether the decision works out as you had hoped or dreamed. But, it is vital that you not regret your decision. The key to not having regrets is to take the time to make a strong and logical decision. Make the best decision at the time with the facts that you have at hand. Everything looks different in the rear view mirror, but you can't worry about that. If you did, you would be paralyzed and never do anything.

Another important analogy that has helped me a lot is the simple ruler. Think about your life as a ruler (or timeline). It represents 80 years. From your birth to your death. I hope 80 years are not enough, but you get the point. Mark out the key points of your life on that ruler. You can place your life events on the ruler, and it will show you several things. First, you can't put small items on there. Second, it will show you what really stands out in your life to date. Third and most importantly, it will put your entire life in perspective. You see life changes so often. You never know what will come next; you must be ready for each phase. Go ahead and do it. *Appendix F* is an example of my life timeline. I can't say that I'm completely happy with the timeline format, but I haven't been able to come up with a better alternative. Maybe you will. If you do, I'd love to hear about it. My e-mail address is in *About the Author* at the end of this book.

I received a book one Christmas that affected the way I think about my life. It was called, *The Wall Chart of World History*. It unfolded and illustrated the history of the entire world on one chart. I thought, "I could do that, too." Although I never actually completed it, I thought a lot about it. Those thoughts affected me and affected my decision-making.

Studying biographies is another activity that helps me keep things in perspective. Reading or watching a biography pulls all these points together. You can see firsthand and without your own emotional bias just how difficult someone's life actually was. On the surface, it may have appeared full of life and without worries, but when you drill down to the specifics, that person's life was just like yours. It was full of events both great and tragic. Your reaction to those events makes you who you are. Watch those biography shows, read that book and see yourself in them.

Perspective is so important to your personal decision-making, and documenting your life will help you establish that perspective.

There is always a way, if you're committed.
—Anthony Robbins

Live with passion.
—Anthony Robbins

It's a funny thing about life; if you refuse to accept less than the very best, you very often get it.
—Unknown

If you reach for the stars, you won't end up with a hand full of mud.
—Leo Burnett

Think of what it can become, not what it is.
—Unknown

Take charge of your attitude. Don't let someone else choose it for you.

Think happy thoughts and you can fly.
—James Barrie

Live with an attitude of gratitude.
—Glen Hopkins

It is not what you are that holds you back; it is what you think you are not.
—Unknown

Your attitude determines your altitude.
—Zig Ziglar

Life is like new fallen snow; every step I take will show.
—Lowri Williams

Everything is possible for him who believes.
—Mark 9:23

I am an optimist. It doesn't seem much use being anything else.
—Unknown

Attitudes are contagious, is yours worth catching?
—Dennis and Wendy Mannering

They never told me I couldn't.
—Tamalyn Dallal

ATTITUDE

Having the right attitude is vital to success. So many times, I have seen very smart and capable people held back by this very "small" difference. It actually isn't small at all. It is everything. If I had to pick one item and one item only as the reason for my success, it would be my attitude. Having a positive attitude has so many advantages; it is almost unfair the assistance it gives you in every aspect of life.

Your attitude affects everything. The way you begin and which path you take at each juncture. Think about this. You make dozens of decisions a day and each one has an effect. It is the law of cause and effect. Think about it as a tree diagram: The decisions affect each part of your life and the path you take. This statement should not scare you about making decisions but rather should help you realize how important it is to let a good attitude influence your decision-making process. This is also a key point about living by your principles and not compromising your basic values. Once you stray away, it is hard to come back. You can also say that you can't ever go back. As true as that is in a literal sense, it doesn't mean you can't get back to a right path, simply that you can't go back to the place or time where you began.

I carry a card in my pocket so that I can follow up on commitments I make or ideas I have during the day. At the top of each index card, I write a saying as a daily reminder or affirmation. Of all the ones that I have used in the past, one stands out: ***There is always a way if you're committed***. It has served me well in situations such as getting cash out of my ownership when I left Excel Resources and in solving and completing the most difficult negotiations.

Expectations are the key to a positive attitude; you control them, as well as whether you attack life or simply let it flow over you. Remember, if you expect the best, you very often get it. What your mind focuses on is what you see. Have you ever noticed say a blue Volkswagen bug that you liked? Then you notice that you see many, many blue Volkswagens? This is a big part of why you should focus on positive things. This hit me again when I was out by our pool cleaning up the second summer in our new house. I was cleaning our tile when I noticed a spot of cement on it. I saw it and popped it off. Then I noticed another then another. They were everywhere. I spent the next several hours popping them off but they were still everywhere. I was stunned. I had admired our pool often and we kept it in good condition. I really liked the glass tile and enjoyed the pool very much. I overlooked the small flaws and didn't even notice them. Once I did, I saw them everywhere. I sat down and really pondered that observation. It was another wake-up call for me to focus on positive things and, if I find I am in a negative state, to change that state. Be careful noticing the negative in a person and not the positive. Those negatives can build and build, and your relationship with that person can change forever.

Here is a very important and moving example of how the right attitude changed the McConnell lives forever. When I was at Excel Resources, I began listening to *The Choice* by Og Mandino on my daily commute. We had quite a collection of his work at the office. I listened to books on tape every day. We were having a difficult time at work and were considering going public with a reverse merger on the American Stock Exchange. A strange series of events led up to it, but Fritz was really engaged and wanted to do it. The company was growing very well but was still barely hanging on by its fingernails and he wanted to take over the day-to-day operations again. That was fine; it was his company, but something with his new friend and advisor wasn't right. I was very uncomfortable with the whole thing. Fritz had also asked me to put up a personal guarantee for the company. This was a request that I couldn't meet. I could not bet my family's financial life on it. It changed my relationship with Fritz significantly. With all of this going on, Og Mandino's book hit me like a lighting bolt. The effect was profound and immediate. It is a book about God and true prioritization. It really seemed to be speaking to me, directly to me. One of my favorite affirmations is, "When the student is ready, the teacher will come." I was ready to hear that message. God was telling me something and I was listening. Within the week of finishing the book, which often moved me to tears, I made the decision to leave Excel and sell my interest back to Fritz so that he could take the company public in the way he believed was right. On that Saturday, we agreed to terms for the buyout and I left the company. I made the negotiations easy; all I wanted was what my contract said I was owed. Not a penny more, not a penny less. I didn't want options in the new company; I wanted the cash that was owed to me. He paid me $256,000 cash and I left. That was a lot of money at that point, but he found a way to write me a check. I was free and believed I had done a great thing for Fritz and for my family.

If there were any doubt that I believe and learned something from affirmations it came true during this buyout. Fritz told me that he couldn't come up with the cash and I told him, "There is always a way, if you're committed." That is my favorite affirmation and one that I look at almost every day—even today. I found so many parts of *The Choice* to be inspirational, including the very reason I am writing this book at all. The main character in the book quit his executive job to be with his family, became a writer of inspirational books and helped millions of people. One part of the book that had the most power was his speech toward the very end. I found it very moving and very true about describing the problems of the world.

I had the opportunity to meet Og Mandino in person. My wife and I saw in the paper that he was coming to speak and we attended. We waited at the end and got a chance to talk with him and he autographed my copy of *The Choice*. I only had it in paperback but it is a prized possession of mine. I also had the chance to tell him a short version of my story and how his book had changed my life. It was great to have the ability to thank him in person. I know that I am one of thousands of people whose lives he has changed for the better. What a gifted person.

Back to *The Choice*. The speech at the end of the book says so much about attitude and choosing a better life through what you believe and acting in a better way, a better attitude, I thought I would insert it to review. Unfortunately, Random House, the publisher of *The Choice*, wanted $1,200 for me to include this brief excerpt in my book. Although I believe very strongly in the power of this speech, I could not pay that amount of money and feel good about it. Instead, I urge you to read it on your own and to feel its impact in your life.

He can because he thinks he can.
—Unknown

Events, small or large, can foster beliefs.
—Anthony Robbins

Man is what he believes.
—Anton Chekov

Whether you believe you can do something or you believe you can't,
you're right.
—Unknown

If you believe in magic, you'll have a magical life.
—Anthony Robbins

Beyond believing is knowing.
—Unknown

Let the fear go, it's just a thought, tell it to pass and move on.
—Unknown

For he who believeth, all things are possible.
—Proverbs 3:5, 6

Suspend disbelief and anything can happen.
—Unknown

Change your thoughts and you can change your habits.
—Unknown

All things are possible for me.
—Unknown

No pessimist ever discovered the secrets of the stars, or sailed to an
uncharted land or opened a new heaven to the human spirit.
—Helen Keller

Champions believe in themselves, even when others do not.
—Unknown

Faith doesn't mean the absence of fear. It means having the energy
to go ahead, right alongside of fear.
—Sharon Salzburg

Believe in something larger than yourself.
—Barbara Bush

THE POWER OF BELIEF

You are successful for a reason. I have often found myself thinking, "I don't get it. I'm not that good or that smart, so why do people think I am?" I think we are our own harshest critics. I have seen this proven repeatedly. Almost everyone is tougher on himself or herself than the boss would be.

I believe in each affirmation listed on the opposite page. Life is truly a matter of perspective. Your levels of optimism and belief change everything. All my professional life I have had the belief that I could do anything. That is not to say that I didn't have doubts or wasn't scared. I'm also not talking about arrogance or over-confidence. I simply believe that I have the capabilities and know that a focused attack on a problem works. Some people look at assignments as problems. I see them more as opportunities and challenges. Think about the difference in your whole approach if you start off not behind or thinking that it can't be done. Some people make a Mount Everest out of a molehill. I remember working on the J-Block problem at Enron, when many very smart people told me that I couldn't possibly solve it. I mean a lot of people. I also didn't have a single person encouraging me to take the job. My first reply was that if they can make peace in the Middle East, I could certainly solve this negotiation.

One of my favorite examples of the power of belief is from Denis Waitley's book, *The Psychology of Winning*. Scientific data stated that a human being was physiologically incapable of running a mile in under four minutes. That study capped, at least mentally, what people thought they could do. Roger Bannister beat the four minutes in a true surprise and broke the myth. A very interesting thing then happened. The four-minute mile was broken many times that same year; amazing the power of belief and holding yourself back. Even in Olympic athletes. Just like the challenge you have in front of you. If you believe you can do it, you can. The approach is so important.

If you have any questions about belief, just look at the statistics on cancer patients. There is a surprising correlation between a person's belief or even the first reaction to hearing the news that they had cancer and their success in beating that cancer. Thousands of patients experience "miraculous" recoveries simply because they believe they will beat the cancer.

There are also many studies about the "placebo" effect on people. Why do so many people have positive reactions to placebo drugs? People can eat a sugar tablet, and yet their illness goes away. People have written many books about this. Find some and read them. This is so important. If you can really understand the power of belief, it can steer your life.

Chapter Two:

Values

We are nothing without our values. These are formed at a very early age and are reinforced by our family, our friends, and our actions. If you have children, you already know how important it is to maintain the core values of your family. Take this role upon yourself; be the leader in your family. Each member will be tested in his or her life, and sometimes the temptation to stray will be very powerful. Your recognition of the importance of solid values and the example you set for your family will help direct them in times of need. Likewise, it is important for you to surround yourself with people who share your values, so you will have a place to turn when you are tested, too.

Value systems are shaped by a great many external influences, and perhaps the most powerful of these is religion. When I began this book, religion was not a primary focus, but I quickly realized that it should be. The entire book is nothing if you don't get this right. As a devout Christian, I like knowing that this life is the opening act. If we have a good life but die without being a Christian and going to heaven, what was the purpose of it all? Think about how ridiculous that would be. As you continue reading this section and others, think about how difficult it would be to uphold the principals presented here without strong Christian values.

Over my life, my church attendance has varied a lot. So many times in my life, I was too busy, or lost interest or simply was too lazy to go to church. It was never for the same reason. I was often able to talk myself out of going and make myself feel just fine about it. Looking back on it and writing this makes me almost chuckle due to my foolishness. Over the years when I did drift away, I returned when there was a void or a real need in my life. Usually it wasn't an obvious sign, I just found that I would start going to church or praying more. I know that God was carrying me through my times when I wasn't focused on God or Christ, as I should have been. It is important. Set a good Christian example.

This entire book is actually all about religion. It is in each chapter. If you look at the affirmations, it all returns to religion and following the principals of God's rules. If you ever are at a loss as to what to do, just think about following the Ten Commandments:

I. Thou shalt have no other gods but me.
II. Thou shalt not make to thyself any graven image, or the likeness of any thing that is in heaven above, or in the earth beneath, or in the water under the earth; thou shalt not bow down to them, nor worship them.
III. Thou shalt not take the Name of the Lord thy God in vain.
IV. Remember that thou keep holy the Sabbath day.
V. Honor thy father and thy mother.
VI. Thou shalt do no murder.
VII. Thou shalt not commit adultery.
VIII. Thou shalt not steal.
IX. Thou shalt not bear false witness against thy neighbor.
X. Thou shalt not covet.

The great commandment from Jesus:

Thou shall love the Lord thy God with all thy heart, with all thy soul, and with all thy mind. This is the first and great commandment. And the second is like unto it: You shall love your neighbor as yourself.

Unfortunately, I couldn't recite them from memory; most people can't. But, find them and write them down.

I remember when people began wearing bracelets that had WWJD on it. It stood for "What Would Jesus Do". A good guideline, I think. I really liked that movement.

Go to church and listen to the sermon. Many times, actually most of the time, my mind wanders off to work, golf, or a long list of other things. I do try to bring myself back to the sermon, though, because I really do believe in the expression that I used earlier in the book. "When the student is ready, the teacher will come." You will hear what you are ready for, what you need to hear in the sermon. It can help you even if it is just one sentence or simple thought. Even if you are drifting to sleep, even if it is just mentally, try to pull yourself back and listen to the preacher. God is trying to tell you something but you have to give him a chance.

Be the spiritual leader of your family. I take this job very seriously. That is not to say that Chris is not religious or constantly doesn't want to go to church; it is just that I take this responsibility as part of my job. I am happy to have that accountability on my shoulders.

If you are ever really having a hard time in your life, just remember one of my favorite bible sayings, "If God is for us, who can be against us?" I think that really says it all. I first learned this while reading the ultimate positive self-help book, *The Power of Positive Thinking* by Norman Vincent Peale.

One other thing I do that helps a great deal is wear a cross around my neck. It is a subtle reminder of why we are here.

In your life, you will have quite a spiritual journey. It will go in so many directions. As I look back, I can be ashamed of some of my journey. I had the road-map and didn't even take the time to read it. I was so foolish at times. I read a very interesting book that also added perspective. It is *The Purpose Driven Life* by Rick Warren. It was a best seller and was very thought provoking. It was also very disturbing. A book like that can really make you reanalyze your entire life and your purpose on the earth. I think it is very good to force yourself out of your comfort zone and deeply reflect on your life. I can tell you that while reading the book I was very shaken up at times and it made me take a deep breath and pray for forgiveness.

If there is any doubt about how things work, just read this as a reminder.

Footprints
—Unknown

One night a man had a dream. He dreamed he was walking along the beach with the Lord. Across the sky flashed scenes from his life. For each scene, he noticed two sets of footprints in the sand; one belonged to him, and the other to the Lord. When the last scene of his life flashed before him, he looked back at the footprints in the sand. He noticed that many times along the path of his life there was only one set of footprints. He also noticed that it happened at the lowest and saddest times in his life. This really bothered him and he question the Lord about it. "Lord, you said that once I decided to follow you, you'd walk with me all the way. But I have noticed that during the most troublesome times in my life, there is only one set of footprints. I don't understand why when I needed you most you would leave me." The Lord replied, "My precious, precious child, I love you and I would never leave you. During your times of trial and suffering, when you see only one set of footprints, it was then that I carried you."

PRAYER POWER

Don't let anyone tell you that praying doesn't matter. I will discuss the guidance I received for going back to Enron after bankruptcy, and in 2005, another event told me a lot.

A grand jury indicted my dear friend Kevin Howard for activities that happened with the Enron Broadband Services (EBS). As the CFO, he was included in the firestorm of blame for anything that happened with EBS. I worked with Kevin twice at Enron and once he was my head of finance while I was president of two pipelines. He was simply outstanding—one of the hardest working, most passionate, and highest integrity people I've ever worked with. He was very innovative and helped our business grow and change. He came up with many creative ways to do business but always in a very ethical and thoughtful way. His trial was coming up and I thought a lot about him. One day at work in my Houston office, it hit me what I could do to help him. I was to pray for him. Not just to pray but also to pray for him right then on my knees in my office. I did and it was very intense. It came to me that I was to do that every day on my knees before I started the day. I was supposed to do that. In fact, I thought if I didn't or if I missed a day, it would hurt him somehow and that my failure would help him go down. In fact, I've never prayed like that before in my life. It was different from all the praying I had ever done before. I kept my promise from that day, and I didn't miss a day for months. After a very long trial, the verdict came out; he got a mistrial and the jury didn't find him guilty of a single charge. In some way, I really feel that my dedication and belief made a real difference. God knew just how committed I was to him, to his innocence and to justice.

Again, don't let anyone tell you this doesn't work. If you believe you are doing the right thing, you should never give up on the power of prayer.

Come unto me, all ye that labor and are heavy laden, and I will give you rest.
—Matthew 11:28

I have been driven to my knees many times because there was no place else to go.
—Abraham Lincoln

The gods favor the bold.
—Ovid

When a man's willing and eager, the gods join in.
—Aeschylus

If God be for us, who can be against us?
—Romans 8:31

Ye have not, because ye ask not.
—James 4:2

Work as if you were to live 100 years; pray as if you were to die tomorrow.
—Benjamin Franklin

Believe that your prayers will be answered. They will be. And prayer is always answered in one of three ways: No, yes, or wait a while.
—L. Ray Smith

We have 35 million laws to enforce the Ten Commandments.
—Unknown

God doesn't make orange juice; God makes oranges.
—Jesse Jackson

Two marks of a holy person; giving and forgiving.
—Unknown

To me, faith is not just a noun but also a verb.
—Jimmy Carter

Bibles that are falling apart usually belong to people who are not.
—Unknown

I can do all things through Christ, which strengthens me.
—Philippians 4:13

Where there is great love there are always miracles.
—Unknown

READ THE BIBLE

In the summer of 2003, I was unemployed and spending a lot of time reflecting on the course of my life. Being off has some very nice advantages. We are always way too busy living life to sit back and enjoy it. The faster the pace of your life is, the more life's events become a blur. I had a conversation with Greg Sharp, a great person and dear friend of mine, and he told me about a great book that he read, called *The Purpose Driven Life.* He was so impacted by it I told him I would try it. It was quite the rage and everyone was talking about it, too. I picked it up at the bookstore and soon discovered its power. This is not a book for wimps, I thought; at least not wimps on commitment. Its basis is around Christ but also around the significance of 40 days in the bible. The book is broken down into 40 short readings and thoughts, but you must stick with it every day for 40 straight days. It was fascinating and I didn't miss a day. The book and resulting relationship with and learning about Jesus and about me had huge effects. In fact, as I am writing this, I believe I need to read the book again. I started in July, and although I did have to fit it into the day sometimes, I usually looked forward to it, and it would put me in good mood when I would think about reading my installment. Some days I would go out to the hammock, lie in the shade and read. I would also start with a prayer for guidance and to have the message reach me deeply and to understand what I was about to read. I am such a believer in the saying, "When the student is ready the teacher will come." I definitely wanted to be a student and have the ultimate teacher fill me with knowledge. Each day made me ponder and ask different questions of myself on parts of my life.

As I was reading the book, Chris and I were also taking Discovery classes at church. The combination of the two activities inspired me to take action. We were in class studying different Bibles when I decided I was ashamed that I had never read the Bible and was so ignorant of a great majority of the book. I made a covenant that it was my time to read the Good Book. We learned in class that it takes only 15 minutes of reading a day and you can read the entire Bible in 1 year. I had read that much each day while reading the *Purpose Driven Life.* I went on a quest to get a good Bible—one that would help me in my quest, not make it tougher. I found a great Bible that a woman in the class had recommended. I bought the Life Application Bible, the new American Standard Version. It is also the same version of text as the Bible we use in the Episcopal Church. The Bible turned out to be a key. It contained bios for significant characters, maps, explanations, history, etc. It helped so much. In fact, I am sure I couldn't have accomplished my mission with out using this Bible. After a long dedication and a lot of time and sometimes-forced commitment, I did it. It was hard and often frustrating, but I did it. I am very proud of this accomplishment.

One of my motivations was actually TV. I watch so much TV, a fact that I am not proud of, and one night a thought came to me. Actually, it was in the form of a dream, almost a vision. I was watching myself. I had passed on and was talking with God. We were talking and I was telling him that I didn't have time to read his book. I had had time each day for most of my life to watch reruns of every episode of my favorite TV show, *Everybody Loves Raymond*, 20 times, but I just didn't have time to read His book, ever! I didn't like that visual. I dedicated myself to rectifying that priority problem.

I feel so good about reading the Bible from cover to cover, and that building block will be part of my personal foundation forever. Make sure you don't reach the "pearly gates" and have to say you didn't have time to read the most important book ever written. The Word of God.

Chapter Three:

Character: Doing the Right Thing

Never, ever go against this. This is different from not knowing what the right call is or what your gut reaction is to something. This is about principles and treating people with respect. I have given many people a great deal of bad and earth-shattering news but I always did so honestly and openly. It is so easy to bail and not give full disclosure or delay the bad news for another day, but it will usually come back and haunt you later.

Living by this is vital. It will treat you right. I once went to a charity event for the Juvenile Diabetes Foundation at which General Norman Schwarzkopf spoke. I picked him up at the airport and had the opportunity to meet and talk with him. At the charity ball, Chris and I also had the chance to talk and get our picture taken with him. His speech was fantastic. He discussed a couple of principles that are vital to leadership and one that cannot ever be compromised. As an example, he cited his first big command at the Pentagon. His boss left for a one-month tour just as he arrived. He was nervous and asked, "What do I do in your absence?" His boss told him to simply do his job and do the right thing. That is very simple but excellent advice. You can never go wrong by doing the right thing. Even if you made the wrong decision or wrong call, you can correct it, and your logic will make it easier to correct or change course.

One situation made a huge impression on me. During the crazy time of the Enron bankruptcy, leadership almost entirely halted real and meaningful communication to the employees. Everyone was worried about liability and saying the wrong thing. It wasn't because of a desire not to communicate, but the lawyers were in total control. It was chaos. On the Friday before the bankruptcy was filed, I decided to have a floor meeting to go through what was probably about to happen. Although I couldn't say things with certainty, the employees had a right to know what we knew and what was about to happen to their lives and families. I told them what I knew about the state of the company. It also gave me a chance to say goodbye and let them know how proud I was to have worked with them and to remind them just how good they really were. The press had made everyone out as dishonest people and it was easy to start believing it. Everyone went home and waited for the next disastrous event. I am so thankful that I did that. The bankruptcy happened faster than expected and instead of filing on Monday and having layoffs on Tuesday it happened on Sunday and we laid everyone off on Monday morning. If I hadn't acted that Friday, I would have had no chance, and I think it was important to everyone and to me. I did what was right.

Doing the right thing sometimes takes more than simply thinking you know what to do. Praying and paying attention can be the answer. In February of 2002, I had such an experience. Jeff McMahon was a good friend of mine and called me to have lunch. Jeff became president of Enron after the bankruptcy. What an incredible and hard job. He came to me and asked me to consider returning to Enron. The company was in trouble, more trouble than people realized it was. The thought of going back to Enron made me sick to my stomach. I couldn't imagine it. I was so sad about the entire thing; I took the collapse and bankruptcy very personally.

Jeff explained that there were two huge problems on the horizon, and they were arriving like a freight train. Days before the bankruptcy, the company selected people considered vital to the organization. The company paid a bonus to these individuals for staying for at least 90 days after the bankruptcy filing. The philosophy was that selected people were vital to keep billions of dollars with the company and not let it melt away. The intention was to manage the businesses properly in a wind-down. It was the overall view that, although the selected people were paid ridiculous sums of money, a huge number of them would walk out on the 91st day and not care what happened to the company after that. Jeff believed it was going to be a terrible day and one that the company may not be able to recover from without giving remaining employees some hope. The other huge issue was the pressure from the credit committee to move the company into Chapter 7 bankruptcy, which is a total liquidation, not reorganization. If a company does that, all the employees and retirees would also lose their health insurance because a Chapter 7 company upon liquidation is gone and treated as if it didn't exist. That means that not only did thousands of people lose their jobs and lose their savings; but also now those same people would lose their health insurance. That prospect made me sick to my stomach. I kept thinking of all of my field employees from Houston Pipeline Company, how many of them were senior citizens, and thus may have serious health issues. How could this happen? I felt like throwing up.

Jeff's idea was to bring me back to the company to run all the unregulated businesses and to help him write a business plan. A good strong business plan could convince the creditors of the value that remained in the company and that Chapter 7 was a bad idea, which would cost a lot of money. He also said that with everyone leaving, my coming back would be a beacon of hope that someone believed in coming out of bankruptcy and that a "good" person was going to help. There was a huge leadership void in the company. It was a lot to ask and I felt the pressure.

I came home and told Chris about it. I was numb. We went through all the positives and negatives. I was perplexed and queasy thinking about it. I needed real gut advice. I decided to do something that would turn out to be big. I took my folding chair out to the lot we had purchased to build our new house (pre-bankruptcy of course). I set up my chair, sat amongst the trees and just thought and prayed. I prayed for guidance and direction. I spent a couple of hours being alone and receptive to my prayers and thoughts, and the answer came to me. I needed to do this. I had been so fortunate in my time at Enron and had a lot of security due to my conservative nature. So many people needed help. I was destined to do this; it didn't matter that I didn't want to. It was the right thing to do. I decided that it also wouldn't be about money. I didn't want any special deals, just my salary. If more money came for doing a good job, good for my family, but that was not going to be my driver. I accepted the job and started work. On my first day, I drove in, parked in the garage and sat in my car for a moment, pondering my walk in. When I did walk in, I was alone; not one person was in the lobby. A building that had always been full of electricity and busy people was now abandoned. The job was going to be difficult both in the task and in emotion. Things had changed. It knew it was the right thing to do, but on that first day, I was questioning myself.

However, doing things for the right reason has consequences. I believe that. I had many positive experiences. One person I didn't even know hugged and thanked me in the elevator. Others simply said with great feeling, "Thanks for coming back." Wow. But, I believe there were more consequences as well. Some of which I never dreamed. I truly believe God watched over me and realized my sacrifice. I think that my coming back, I hope for the right reasons, also had the greatest impact of all. The investigations and witch-hunt for all the "bad" people at Enron would become larger than anyone could have expected. It was a scary time. I would eventually pray as hard as I had ever prayed for some of my friends going through hell and accused of terrible things. Those prayers would mainly be around the topic of praying for real justice to happen. But, as for me, I never talked with anyone at the FBI, department of Justice or the SEC. Never. I was literally the only one on the Enron executive committee who can say that. I believe that my decision to return had something to do with that. No good deed goes unrecognized. If I ever needed a reminder to do the right thing all the time, I believe I got it.

There is one more example that may be at the top of my life lessons when it comes to doing the right thing in normal, day-to-day decision-making. Writing this story today brings goose bumps to me:

It was spring 2001. Chris and I had decided to exercise some Enron stock options and pull some money off the table. I had received new stock options earlier in the year and thought I would be smart and continue to diversify our portfolio. We decided to take some big dollars out of our large Enron position and make $1 million and put it into our other investments. I made several calls in the morning to exercise some identified options. I was very busy and was interrupted many times while trying to make the calls. I was frustrated, but I just couldn't find the time to complete it. It is not easy to exercising options, as you must confirm that you don't have any insider information by getting approval from Enron's general counsel or securities counsel who must then confirm with the broker that it is okay to make a trade. I was frustrated when I went to the Monday morning executive committee meeting at 11 a.m. In that meeting Ken Rice, the CEO of Enron Broadband Services, announced that there were big problems with the Blockbuster transaction and their ability to deliver movies and that we might have to kill the deal. That was big and shocking news. When I heard it, I just put my head on the table. My ability to exercise was over. This was true insider information. I was disappointed but didn't think much about it again other than having to tell Chris that we didn't make a bunch of money as we had expected. I had also planned to take her out to celebrate. Making that much money is a shocking and life-changing event. Little did I know what was coming later in the year. If I had quietly gone ahead and completed the transaction as I could have done, I would probably be in jail today and I would have deserved it. The most important thing is that it didn't even cross my mind to do that. It is also important to step back in time. This was all before a bunch of corporate scandals and insider trading and CEO investigations.

This is why doing the right thing and acting with integrity is so important. Subconscious, day-to-day decision-making makes you who you are. If I were to try to pick one thing that led me to avoid falling under any investigation or suspicion it would have to be that. There is also another lesson that I learned here: Giving people the benefit of the doubt and not convicting someone on circumstantial evidence. What do I mean? This: What if I had gotten through on the call that morning? It would have been a complete coincidence that I had exercised options that morning, but I don't think a single person in America would have believed me. I had actually worked for Ken Rice in a previous position. No one in the world would have believed that I didn't have some inside information and had acted on it. I hope that doing what is right would have saved me again, because I am sure I would have immediately called the general counsel and told him what happened. That also gives me goose bumps.

Remember: If you are in a job where you can't do the right thing, look for a new job. You are in control. If you chose not to, it is up to you and you are making the choice. It will have consequences but that is okay. If it is the right thing to do, do it.

A president's hardest task is not to do what is right, but to know what is right.
—Lyndon Baines Johnson

Nurture your mind with great thoughts.
—Benjamin Disraeli

Ability may get you to the top but it takes character to keep you there.
—Unknown

Your true character is revealed by the clarity of your convictions, the choices you make and the promises you keep.
—*Successories, The Essence of Character*

The game of life is the game of boomerangs. Our thoughts, deeds and words return to us sooner or later, with astounding accuracy.
—Florence Shinn

Character is doing what's right when nobody's looking.
—J.C. Watts

Every action triggers long-term consequences.
—Unknown

The true meaning of life is to plant trees under whose shade you do not expect to sit.
—Nelson Henderson

There's no pillow as soft as a clear conscience.
—French Proverb

Show class, have pride, and display character. If you do, winning takes care of itself.
—Paul Bryant

Character isn't inherited. One builds it daily by the way one thinks and acts.
—Helen Gahagan Douglas

The Golden Rule applies, at all times, in all things, in all places.
—Matthew 7:12

Always try to treat people just a little bit better than they treat me. That could be the key to world peace.
—Unknown

Integrity is not negotiable.
—Various

KEEP YOUR PROMISES

Your word is your bond.

You should keep your promises. I have fun examples of this, from back in 1996 when I was on my London assignment. My wife and had gone to the theater late one night, but Claire came bounding down the stairs when we got home. She was five, so we were very surprised to see her up, and so was the sitter. Claire informed me that she had had a nice chat with "Mr. Ken." I looked at her with a surprised expression and turned to Chris. She had no idea either. I said, "Mr. Ken? Who called?" The babysitter didn't know anything about it. "Mr. Ken" she said with a frustrating tone. "Mr. Lay!? Ken Lay called?" I said. "Yes, Mr. Ken," Claire replied proudly. I about fell over. I said, "So did he leave a number or a message?" Claire replied, "No we just talked." I about fell over, again. "What did you say?" All Claire would say was, "We had a nice long talk." My knees were getting weak. I told myself to be calm and that I would figure out what he wanted and call him in the states tomorrow. I asked Claire, very casually, "How long did you talk to Mr. Ken?" "About 30 minutes," she replied. Thirty minutes! My career flashed in front of my eyes. Thirty minutes with Ken Lay, who was about to attend the World Economic Forum in Davos, Switzerland and deliver a speech! "What did you talk about?" I asked. "It's a secret," she said. "It's a secret it was between Mr. Ken and me." I think I actually died right then. How could my career be over so soon?

She then turned and went to bed and left me weak-kneed and shaken. I did talk to Ken the next day and he backed her story to a tee. He told me that they had quite a conversation but it was strictly between them. Flustered, I asked again and he told me not to worry, but that it was a private conversation. Incredible. To this day, I still don't know what they talked about. I asked him many times and even Chris tried it. He kept his word. I respected him for that even now, as I am writing this. That is the Ken Lay I know, and he is not the man who ended up convicted in shame as a corporate bad guy. I want to be known as someone who keeps his word, just as Ken always did.

We are our choices.
—Unknown

Not to decide is to decide.
—Unknown

Days are scrolls; write on them what you want to be remembered.
—Bachya ibn Pakuda

Time flies. It's up to you to be the navigator.
—Robert Orben

The essential conditions of everything you do must be choice, love and passion.
—Nadia Boulanger

Losers take chances. Winners make choices.
—Unknown

I discovered I always have choices and sometimes it's only a choice of attitudes.
—Unknown

There are two primary choices in life: To accept conditions as they exist, or accept the responsibility for changing them.
—Denis Waitley

Your destiny is not a matter of chance; it's a matter of choice.
—Unknown

If you do not change you can become extinct.
—Spencer Johnson

When it comes to change, people are like plants; they are either growing or dying.
—Unknown

A mind is like a rubber band, once stretched it never returns to its original shape.
—Unknown

It's our choices … that show what we truly are, far more than our abilities.
—J.K. Rowling

If you can't explain it to your mother or grandmother, don't do it.
—Carl Sandburg

CHOICES

You are your choices. God gave you your genes, your makeup, your potential. However, it is what you do with that gift that makes the difference. Your choices define you. They are a series of decisions that make up who you are and what you really stand for. I've talked a lot about actions speaking louder than words, and the rubber meets the road right here. You make thousands of choices in your lifetime, some very small and insignificant and others small but life changing. The key is what drives your unconscious choices and daily selections. Your foundation, belief systems and everything addressed in this book has an influence.

Your environment also obviously influences you, but your reactions within that environment define you. I read a story about a finance guy who worked for Enron in Europe and the slant of the story was that even though he was convicted of several felonies including stealing, fraud and embezzling from the company, he was just doing what the environment of dishonesty around him was doing. I couldn't believe my eyes as I was reading it. Not only did I know many of the people over in that office and that the statement was flatly not true, but also it was attempting to excuse his behavior and pass on accountability to others, even though he was tried and convicted of committing felonies. He was going to prison, which he fully deserved and earned. He had choices and he made them. He made very bad and carefully considered choices. A person is accountable for those choices and, even if he or she makes a mistake, must live with the consequences.

You should not fear this. Your core foundation is very important here. You will do fine if you have the right moral beliefs and core values. They will guide you through. If you make bad choices, you can usually change them later if they don't work out. The crucial step here is to make the choice in the first place.

Chapter Four:

Outlook

HAVE A SENSE OF HUMOR

You don't stop laughing because you grow old; you grow old because you stop laughing.
—Michael Pritchard

You can't take yourself too seriously, although it is easy to do. If you are so intense that you aren't laughing all the time, or at the very least, every day, do something about it. This has never been a problem for me. I make sure that I do silly things or watch silly things. It is hard to be overly serious when you do that. No one likes to be embarrassed, but it is okay to laugh at yourself, even in front of others. This is different from negative self-talk. Being self-effacing in a light way is okay and can have some positive effects on you and everyone around you.

ALLOW YOURSELF TO BE INSPIRED

If you believe in magic, you'll have a magical life.

It is so easy to be caught up in the day-to-day events of living. Weeks and even months can pass while you simply go through the responsibilities of the day. Sometimes you need a break, or you need to be refreshed.

You should allow yourself to be inspired and moved. Sometimes you just need to feel better or get yourself out of the blues—or simply rejuvenated. This is also a lot easier than getting away for a vacation. One technique I use, whether to help me get into a better mood, if there is nothing on TV or I don't feel like doing anything, is to watch some of my favorite scenes from movies. Here are a few of my favorite inspirations from movies.

The first is the last scene in *Indiana Jones and the Last Crusade*. I begin when Indy is captured just outside the cave. He is forced to help the Nazis find the Holy Grail and save his father at the same time. Indiana must use his intellect and faith to accomplish the almost impossible. But, the best part is at the end of his trials to reach the place of the grail. He must make a leap of faith, which appears to be his certain death. As he is pondering the decision he hears his dad's voice in his mind saying, "you must believe." He does believe; and he doesn't die. There are so many lessons in the last 20 minutes of that movie: You must believe in God; God suddenly brings surprises, even eternal life; human nature can so easily decay; Jesus is so humble that the cup giving eternal life is so simple and not ornate; God's power to heal and that there are times to "let it go." I have goose bumps while writing this. Go watch this part of the movie and let the movie flow though you and feel the power of it.

My other most commonly watched scene, which I can't believe hasn't simply worn out, is from *Superman*. *Superman* is one of my favorite movies of all time—if not my very favorite (although I do have many favorites). However, one scene touches me especially. Clark Kent is turning 18 and he is "called" by a buried green crystal that was originally found with him. Shortly after this, his mother looks out over a field of wheat at sunrise and sees Clark, way out in the field. She goes to him, and he tells her with great emotion that he must leave and find his destiny. We all have those times in our lives, and they are pivotal moments. The music is another key here. John Williams, my very favorite composer (yes he also did all of the Indiana Jones and Star Wars films, to name just a few) provided music that also set the scene. It is truly beautiful, at least it is to this hopeless romantic who always wanted to be a nice person and help others.

Another movie that won world acclaim was *Saving Private Ryan*. Chris and I first saw this movie in Anchorage, Alaska while waiting all day for a flight back to Houston after our cruise. We watched the movie and burst into tears. The movie was disturbingly graphic and the first of its kind in reality war movies, but that has nothing to do why I was so moved. At the very end of the movie, Private Ryan, who was now an old man visiting the cemetery of his fallen comrades in WWII, broke down and cried. His wife came running to his side and he asked her, "Was I a good man?" You see, when the main character died trying to save him, he said as he was dying in Ryan's arms, "Earn this."

This scene moved me so greatly because I want to be the kind of man that made a real difference in people's lives, the kind of man who will leave my mark on the world as a good father, husband and person. So many people waste their lives away.

Another movie that actually caused my greatest weeping scene in a theater was *Field of Dreams*. In this great film, a man is moved to build a ball field out of his cornfield under the inspiration of "If you build it, they will come." Two things moved me greatly in this movie. The first is that Kevin Costner's character, Ray Kinsella, gets to see his dad in a new light; they had a bad relationship during Ray's childhood. My tears came from the fact that my wife Chris had never seen my "true" dad—before bankruptcy and the self-inflicted punishment it brought upon him. I have a great relationship with my dad, but that point bubbled up during the movie. The other very touching scene that still moves me is at the end of the movie. Not the actual great ending itself, where God speaks though Ray's daughter, but when Moonlight Graham, the doctor, gives up the life he always wanted as a baseball player to come back and save Ray's child from choking. I want to be that kind of man, a man with no regrets and a man who does the right thing.

The last one I will mention is from a very little known movie called *Joshua*. It is about Christ coming back in modern times. It is a quiet and nice little movie but the ending really moves me. Joshua goes to the Vatican; he is in trouble and visits the Pope. This scene and the scene before it that sets it up are so moving because they are so simple and the message is so uncomplicated. Jesus is so humble and able to be moved before a mere man. His message was so unselfish, he warned the Pope to remind people that he loves them. That was it. No laundry list of items to do, no punishments to deal out for sin; just tell people that I love them. It speaks volumes.

I could remain forever on this topic, but I wanted to share a few of my moving and inspirational events with you. What are yours? Whatever they are—whether from a movie, song, book or a memory—cherish them and make sure that on occasion you recall them and remind yourself about your life.

Remembering great events or moving things is never a bad idea. It is always time well spent. Part of being inspired is listening to yourself and internal inspiration and then taking action. If you follow your inspiration you will be successful and at peace with yourself.

BE PATRIOTIC

Don't ever hesitate to be patriotic. I've displayed our flag for years and enjoy it every day. You don't really think about it every day, but I believe that internally or subconsciously you do. I am so proud to be an American and want to let people know. Our freedom is something we take for granted every day. Every day. Take advantage of our national holidays to reflect and think about our freedoms.

Think about the sacrifices that people made by being soldiers. Think about people and families who paid the ultimate price for you to have a great life and opportunity for everything you have. When someone dies on the battlefield, his or her family changes forever. There are wives, children who will never be the same. Please think about that. Rent war movies. Read books about our founding fathers, read about what normal Americans did for you and for all of us. Thank a soldier. Be appreciative in your heart. To remind myself of what these people have done for me, I occasionally watch WWII programs on the History Channel. I also find myself reaching for some of the classic movies that address what these brave people did for us. Movies like *Patton* or *The Longest Day* are two of my favorites. Interestingly, I notice I do this around military holidays or the Fourth of July. Of course, this isn't a coincidence.

Don't be afraid to have tears in your eyes every time you hear *The Star Spangled Banner*. Sing the *National Anthem* every time. Put your hand over your heart and feel the sacrifices people have made for you. Do it out of respect. Do it even when you don't feel like it. Think about all the countries of the world that are poor or in conflict. The fact that you were born in the USA and into a good family is pure luck on your part. You could be in the middle of an African village. You could be living on the streets of Bombay, India.

Don't let people tell you that you shouldn't pray in school. Don't let people tell you that you shouldn't be forced to say the Pledge of Allegiance in school. Don't let people tell you that it is okay to burn the flag. It's not okay. Don't ever do it and don't ever believe that it is okay. People argue that it is their "right" to do it, which is actually true, but it doesn't mean you should do it. Think about the title of this book.

God bless America.

Count your blessings, not your blemishes.
—Unknown

Want to get rich quickly? Count your blessings.
—Unknown

Gratitude is the sign of noble souls.
—Aesop

Gratitude is not only the greatest of all the virtues, but the parent of all the others.
—Cicero

Reflect upon your present blessings, of which every man has many; not on your past misfortunes, of which all men have some.
—Charles Dickens

Gratitude is the most exquisite form of courtesy.
—Jacques Maritain

Now and then it's good to pause in our pursuit of happiness and just be happy.
—Unknown

Gratitude is a debt, which usually goes on accumulating like blackmail; the more you pay, the more is extracted.
—Unknown

O Lord my God, I will give thanks to thee forever.
—Psalms 30:12

Ingratitude is sooner or later fatal to its author.
—Twi Proverb

The triple A formula for experiencing happiness begins by accepting the moment, appreciating it and adapting to its opportunities.
—Dale Carnegie

Success is getting what you want; happiness is wanting what you get.
—Dale Carnegie

Saying "thank you" is more than good manners. It is good spirituality.
—Alfred Painter

The hardest arithmetic to master is that which enables us to count our blessings.
—Eric Hoffer

ATTITUDE OF GRATITUDE

People miss the point so easily and so often. We are all so cognizant of what we don't have or what someone else is getting, we miss the point. We should focus on and appreciate what we have—not what we don't have. It is a matter of the wrong focus and lack of appreciation. We should live with an attitude of gratitude. There have been many studies on this and they found that people who appreciate and are thankful live longer and are healthier and certainly more balanced. Many years ago, I even followed an exercise from the book *Unlimited Power,* by Anthony Robbins, and made a list of all the things for which I was thankful. If I really did my job right, the list would have been pages and pages long. People focus on their blemishes, not their blessings. Think about how sad that really is. Without a doubt in my being, I believe that if we would truly appreciate what we have, everyone would be so much better off.

I certainly fall into the trap of wishing or coveting something from time to time. I really try to appreciate our lives and my situation, but I slip occasionally. God also knew that humankind would struggle with this that is why he addressed coveting and even made it a commandment. On occasion I get hit between the eyes and see someone who is really struggling, or I catch myself wishing for something that is really stupid or over the top, and then I get slapped back into reality and remember why I should be so thankful. Once, while staring at a new Mercedes convertible with longing eyes I suddenly looked past it and saw a homeless man in the same view. I was moved and ashamed at my desire for excess when I had so much.

Actually, I did write a new list during a business trip on which I was updating this book. I was on my way to Quebec, Canada and I listed 60 items in a "brainstorming" method. It was a great exercise and made me feel good instantly. I added a few other items again later during that trip. When you make your own list, some of the items won't make you very proud because they are materialistic and may sound shallow. That is all right. It shows you how thankful you should be because you have so much that you even include many smaller or relatively insignificant things that simply make you happy. My car does make me happy, so why not put it down on the list. I guess it isn't unusual because we are truly a materialistic society. But, don't forget the things so many of us take for granted; our health, the health of our kids and loved ones, our freedom, etc.

I did an exercise with Karen Flynn, my sister-in-law, many years ago. I asked her to think about this and come up with a list of things she was grateful for to review each morning. She could hardly come up with anything. I mean she only had a handful of things on her list. It really showed her true state of mind. I was very saddened by that. I decided to help her the next day and put together a very long list. And, that was at a time when our relationship was strained and I was very frustrated with her, yet I could still do it easily.

Make your own list. Then look around at people in a crowd. I can assure you that you will add many items to it and get back on your knees and thank God repeatedly. Not taking even the smallest things for granted will add to your life. Go ahead and make a list. Review it on occasion. If you are having a hard time, put it up on your mirror or a place you will see it every day and watch the result. Do this often in your life. In fact, as I am writing this, I realize I need to do it again. To give an example and get you started, I have included my own list as Appendix A.

Take an action step. Stop right now and begin your list. If you can't or don't want to stop reading; at least stop and think about this for a minute.

Real optimism sees the negatives but accentuates the positives.
Real optimism has reason to complain but prefers to smile.
Real optimism is exposed to the worst but expects the best.
Real optimism knows about difficulties but believes they can be over-come.
—William Arthur Ward

The bigger the crisis, the bigger the opportunity.
—Unknown

When I look into the future, it's so bright, its burns my eyes.
—Unknown

No sense being pessimistic. It wouldn't work anyway.
—John Robb

I'm so optimistic I'd go after Moby Dick in a rowboat and take the tartar sauce with me.
—Zig Ziglar

Positive anything is better than negative nothing.
—Elbert Hubbard

By focusing on positive, healthy motivations and letting the more neg-ative ones pass, you can purify the source of your imaginative power.
—Denis Waitley

Opportunity's favorite disguise is trouble.
—English Proverb

Success is not getting to top—but how you bounce on the bottom that counts.
—Unknown

I'm a pessimist about probabilities; I'm an optimist about possibilities.
—Lewis Mumford

This is the best day the world has ever seen. Tomorrow will be better.
—Unknown

If you are not a positive influence in my life, you are not in my life.
—Unknown

Dwelling on the negative simply contributes to its power.
—Shirley MacLaine

OPTIMISM

What can I say about optimism and its complete power over life? Being an optimist is everything. If you really have this belief in your approach to everyday life, not only will you be happier but you will be more successful, too. Seeing the glass half full, versus half empty changes your approach to every single situation.

In fact, giving the gift of optimism to our children is a top priority. I know that we are making head way because when I tuck Michael and Claire in for bed I always say, "Have a good day tomorrow," and they always answer, "I will." They know and expect to have a great day. That it is theirs for the taking. They don't have any idea what an advantage that will bring them later in life. If someone truly approaches life in such a way, he or she will have a better life. Moreover, building Claire's self-esteem, in particular, was a real priority because the more we read in the parenting books, the more Chris and I learned how poor most girls' or women's self esteem actually is or becomes over time. It was such a big factor that we took classes to learn how to develop that in Claire, and I bought a cassette series from Dr. Denis Waitley, *How to Build Your Child's Self-Esteem* which had a great impact on how we raised our children.

All of my career I took on scary positions, assignments or tasks. But I knew I could do them or at least give them everything I had. Imagine starting every day knowing what you can do, not what you can't do. What a huge difference. It is almost unfair as to how much easier and how much nicer my life is.

Being optimistic doesn't mean that you don't see or feel negative or depressed at times. It means you will get through it and that a bad day or bad event is simply that: A bad day or bad event. It will pass and, a good thing will come along soon.

I once read something else that had a big impact on me. Someone, it may have been Anthony Robbins, said that a person should have a goal to be the most optimistic person in the room. It has another unexpected benefit. Being an optimist also has a tendency to make you popular. Who doesn't want to be around someone who is positive? Someone that brings people down seldom gets included. Some of the smartest and most capable people at Enron wanted to occasionally get together and talk about a problem or about life. Until recently, I never really understood why they did that.

Another benefit is the opportunity to help people, really help them. People have invited me to so many lunches, meetings or calls in which they really wanted my opinion on a subject or my views on a situation. A negative person is easily stuck in problems and needs help getting through tough situations. I had a dear friend who comes to mind with respect to this. While I was in London, one of my fiends was a great person named Rich Dimichele. He was a lawyer who was very smart and had a powerful commercial mind. His general approach to life was definitely more pessimistic than mine, and I think his legal training added to that perspective. Occasionally, Rich would drop by and ask if we could go to lunch and talk. Often we would take a walk to the McDonalds by Victoria Station, which wasn't too far from our office at Four Millbank. We would talk and brainstorm; Rich would share ideas and test assumptions, and we would always have a fun conversation. I would share my thoughts as well, because he had a great thought process and I valued his perspective. The conversation was always stimulating, and I think we really helped each other. In addition, we shared some interesting times.

I am proud that people consider me a big optimist. Make an impact. Think about your influence.

The quality of a person's life is in direct proportion to their commitment.
—Vince Lombardi

Hold tight to your heart's desire, never, never let it go; let nobody fool you into giving it up too soon.
—Unknown

What counts is not necessarily the size of the dog in the fight—it's the size of the fight in the dog.
—Dwight D. Eisenhower

I am more afraid of an army of 100 sheep led by a lion than an army of 100 lions led by a sheep.
—Charles-Maurice de Talleyrand

Every production of a genius must be the product of enthusiasm.
—Benjamin Disraeli

Whatever you attempt, go at it with spirit.
—David Starr Jordan

Heart is what separates the good from the great.
—Michael Jordan

Passion persuades.
—Anita Roddick

I never had the ambition to be something. I had the ambition to do something.
—Unknown

Nothing is impossible to the willing heart.
—Abraham Lincoln

Passions are the gales of life.
—Alexander Pope

Nothing is so contagious as enthusiasm: It moves stones, it charms brutes. Enthusiasm is the genius of sincerity and truth accomplishes no victories without it.
—Bulwer Lytton

Plunge boldly into the thick of life.
—Johann Wolfgang von Goethe

Every calling is great when greatly pursued.
—Oliver Wendell Holmes, Jr.

LIVE WITH PASSION

I first heard this phrase from Anthony Robbins in his book, *Unlimited Power*. That book had an enormous effect on me and was the first that I ever highlighted and outlined outside my university studies. Passion persuades. The impact is huge. If you really believe in something, people can tell, and they want to be a part of it. Passion attracts people like a magnet. People want to be part of something important, something to believe in, some kind of cause. I have always been able to get enthusiastic about many parts of life. It comes naturally to me and it has helped in all of my various positions. Even if I didn't have any experience with a particular job, I was always ready to tackle it and was pumped about what we could do.

Passion is contagious. Even a real skeptic can pick up the pace without conscious thought. People walk faster, work harder and enjoy work more when they have something to believe in.

The passion has to be real. People can tell if you aren't genuine. If you are living a façade people will know it. There are times that you have to "act" more positive than you feel, especially when you are down or having a bad day, but that is not the same thing. You can sometimes put yourself back in the mood.

Another important aspect of living with passion is to do only the things that you believe in. If you are doing a job that you have issues with or a job that you don't enjoy, it's up to you to move and do something different. That is not to say that there aren't times that we must do things to earn a living or support the family. I believe that if you have passion for what you do, you will be successful. Matching belief and passion and liking your job is a key to being successful.

When I left Enron, for the second time after the bankruptcy, Jeff Donahue told me something at our goodbye lunch that really hit me. He is a brilliant person and I respect his views. He warned me about taking a job in the private equity sector. He explained that I needed a cause or to help people and not just to make money, even if it is a bunch of money. I think he is right. Making money is great but it is not what life is all about. It is hard to be passionate about making money. Besides, isn't living with passion a better way to live?

Change is inevitable. Change is constant.
—Benjamin Disraeli

Change not only continues, but its speed increases.
—Unknown

Human beings, by change, renew, rejuvenate ourselves; otherwise we harden.
—Johann Wolfgang von Goethe

Change yourself; change your future.
—Unknown

Which is stronger; my urge to grow or my resistance to change?
—Unknown

Change your thoughts and change the world.
—Norman Vincent Peale

If you can't change your fate, change your attitude.
—Amy Tan

If you are a dinosaur in changing times, you too will become extinct.
—Unknown

Times change, and we change with them.
—Latin Proverb

Think about the following lessons from *Who Moved my Cheese?*

Change Happens: They keep moving the cheese.

Anticipate Change: Get ready for the cheese to move.

Monitor Change: Smell the cheese often so you know when it is getting old.

Adapt to change quickly: The quicker you let go of old cheese, the sooner you can enjoy new cheese.

Change: Move with the cheese.

Enjoy Change! Savor the adventure and enjoy the taste of new cheese!

Be ready to change quickly and enjoy it again and again: They keep moving the cheese.

CHANGE

Change is inevitable: Be ready and actually welcome and drive it. It happens every day in some respect. People really fear change. That might be okay if it didn't happen often or didn't have much of an effect on our lives. But it does. Hiding from it or spending your life trying to avoid it simply doesn't work. Embrace it and manage it. You really don't have any choice at all. Don't let change simply affect you; take charge of it.

In 2000, we went on a summer vacation to a dude ranch that didn't have any TV, faxes, phones or newspapers. The chance to clear my head and get my priorities back in line was great for me. I am sure that is one of the key reasons that Chris selected this particular dude ranch. I had brought along a very popular book of the day, *Who Moved My Cheese,* by Dr. Spencer Johnson. It had a very strong effect on me in many ways. The book was brilliantly written and very simply put. It really taught some valuable lessons about how to approach life and change. It also helped inspire me to write this book. I had the basic idea of my book in mind but the *Cheese* book inspired me to do it and proved that value could come from something simple and short. As I sat back and thought about the lessons contained in this simple story, it made me realize how very important it was. I have read many management books and have been fascinated with what so-called "experts" say is the path to be an excellent manager or leader. So many are very long and tedious, but more than that, I get very frustrated that the concepts they introduce are completely impossible to implement. I've described many as books of mental masturbation. A harsh expression but one I believe fits.

Cheese was exactly the opposite. It is required reading in our house on a regular basis. While working on an early draft of this book, I was inspired into action about it with my children. I first gave it to my daughter Claire, who was 12 at the time. She enjoyed the story and we talked a lot about which character she was and why the little people got into so much trouble and how they over-thought everything. I was so happy I had had her read it. I then took it to my nine-year-old son Michael and read it to him. He also enjoyed the story, was clearly able to get the lessons, and we discussed the book at every stopping point. Yes, this is a great book. I don't just mean it inspired me, I mean that it moved me to action. When I finished reading the book for the first time, I got my laptop and began writing this. I started my book right then. The choice of going to **that** dude ranch and bringing **that** particular book really did have a huge effect on our lives. See how choices have a big effect and take you in a new direction? *Cheese* is a book that you should read at different times of your life.

I read another very interesting book, called *The New New Thing* by Michael Lewis. It was a fascinating read. It is the story of the infamous Jim Clark of Silicon Valley and how he was so obsessed with change that he felt it was vital in order to keep himself sharp. He was convinced that in this technology world if he didn't constantly move forward and create new products and services, that he would be killed by the competition. He was so obsessed with it that he even changed his swimming pool constantly just to make sure that he was never comfortable and was constantly in a state of change. This is an extreme example, but he had a point. I certainly didn't agree with everything he wrote, but it worked for him. I can't imagine being part of his family.

When I became CEO of Global Technology, I was so over my head, and when I read this book, I realized just how crazy our competition was and how different the technology world was from the energy sector. It kept me sharp, and I moved much quicker in everything I did or we did as an organization. That book had a huge effect on the company by setting the tone for how I attacked the much-needed changes within the IT world at Enron.

My life changed so significantly it was hard to imagine when I took the job. On my very first day, Jeff Skilling and signed a $1 billion commitment with the Number 2 person at IBM, Sam Palmasano. When he and I executed the agreement he asked me how long I had been in the technology world. I told him, "Well it would be about eight hours now." He said, "Hold on, you mean on your very first day, you fly to the corporate headquarters of IBM in Armonk, New York and sign this deal? Wow, I can't wait to tell this story. Well, welcome to the industry!" We had a nice dinner, and I learned that he was a great person. He would soon replace Lou Gerstner as CEO of IBM. That story was actually just the beginning. In the first 10 days on the job, I met with six billionaires. This was change.

The McConnell life story has been a successful story of change and not being afraid, well being afraid, but not letting it stop us from living or making big changes or decisions.

Chapter Five:

Achievement

We feel defined by our achievements, good or bad. For such an important element of our lives, many people spend very little time thinking about what they wish to achieve before they set out to achieve it. Writing goals and objectives is vital to becoming successful no matter how you define success. If you don't know where you are going, any road will get you there. Goals are like magnets. They focus the mind and have enormous influence. Their power is amazing. Studies have proven this again and again. Your subconscious mind is a very important thing. In fact, I believe it is one of the most important ways goal and objectives work. Your mind is thinking about what you want to achieve even if it is on a subconscious level; or better said, especially since it is on a subconscious level. I have used goals successfully in my personal and business life. Both have helped me enormously. In fact, they are one of, if not the primary driver of my success.

People have written many books about how to set goals. I suggest you go to the bookstore, look at several and see if one in particular hits you. Then give it a try. One afternoon, even if your first attempt is in front of the TV, begin to make your list. There are many exercises to help you get started. You can look for magazine articles or books to get some help. There is no lack of information out there. That alone should tell you something about it.

I have personal, family, financial, business and materialistic goals, including pages and pages of ideas and things to think about, at the very least. I've learned so many lessons using this technique. One of the most interesting was forced upon me in business back in 1987. I put down some goals and objectives through a series of conversations with my boss Don Parsons, who was the vice president of Gas Supply and one of the company leaders at Florida Gas. It was an informal process that we later discovered should have been formal. Through conversation, Don gave me a set of tasks and ideas, and I used them to focus on what I should be working on. By the end of the year, I had accomplished all of them. Don discovered that he had never officially given me the list, but I had accomplished the items anyway because of my commitment to my goals. I had made up the list during the year, and it matched his almost perfectly. It wasn't intentional or formal, but it sharpened my focus—which was vital—and it made me very successful. It was the beginning of a great career at a great company.

I also learned another lesson of goals and their power one vacation. I wrote out a whole series, five pages long, of goals in different categories of my life. They included family, personal, work, spiritual and material goals. Under each heading, I had bullet points of important items to accomplish the goals. For example, under "to be a great dad" I had sub points like: To raise good kids which then had ideas like: Read books, talk to Chris, discuss with other parents, review Claire's work, review reference material on child rearing, spend more time at home and tell and show you like and love them. It was something to use as a guide and make sure that I had a path to accomplish something that was important to me. I originally did this in the early 1990s. I developed this list and looked at it occasionally but then I put it in a drawer for a couple of years. Later, I found it and discovered that I had followed many of the items on the list and had accomplished most of them. I am convinced that if I hadn't gone through this process and put these items out there, along with how to accomplish them, I would never have thought of them much less done almost all of them.

It is also important to include detail in your goal setting. Be specific and the more specific the better. If you want to live in a special house someday, list out the items to be included in the house. You will be amazed at what you discover. To illustrate the point, I've included my goals as Appendix B.

BUILDING YOUR PERSONAL BOARD
OF DIRECTORS

This has been very important to the success and, frankly, survival of our family. Do you have a personal board? You especially need a financial expert, a family CFO. I also turn to several friends that have great skills and they provide assistance in my family's life. They don't necessarily know that I take their advice this strongly but they have an enormous effect on our lives. I have always asked the best and the brightest for help, advice or thoughts on a tough problem. So many people don't practice this. I find that many smart people simply have a hard time asking for help or advice. Much less somehow show that they might need any help ever. I would rather solve a big problem. Help someone by giving the best advice rather than worry if I did it only on my own.

We have a family CFO, as well as a resource for general business and financial advice.

Jonny Jones, my best friend and college roommate provides not only general business but also grounding and basic life advice. Jonny is a solid person and a very successful oilman. The oil business is in his genes. He is a third generation oilman and his family's company goes back into the 1920s. His whole family has had an enormous influence on me. In fact, in my senior year at OU, the oil business was falling apart, and that is an understatement. It was actually going into a multiyear depression. Jonny's father, Jon Rex Jones, encouraged me to stick with my major and the oil business. Boy was he right! I believe that I very well may have changed my major without his impact. Mr. Jones is a true giant in the oil business. I really admire him and his family. He and his wife Ann are like a second set of parents to me; they have a wonderful marriage and are very grounded. This is even more amazing when considered with the fact that they are extremely wealthy and live in a world of influence.

My brother Mark, of course, is someone I turn to all the time for advice. He is more than my brother and closest confidant; he has been elected to my board, as well.

I have many others on my "Board of Advisors." Objective thought is important. It works for corporations—why would it not work for your own personal situation?

FINANCES

A penny saved is a penny earned.
—Benjamin Franklin

It is safe to say that I am a conservative. I've always been a saver and it has paid off. Watching the amount of debt you have is very important. Of course, there are times to go into debt or extend yourself occasionally, but you should always make it a decision with an exit strategy. Opportunities do come up or appear at tough times and you may decide to take advantage of a situation. If you do go into debt, make a plan for taking it off your books and solving the problem. Making a sacrifice to compensate for going into debt also makes you appreciate what you bought and how you saved for it.

It is always better to be biased for cash and paying it off. We were very careful not to over-extend ourselves on our credit cards and, if we did need to borrow for a couple of months, we didn't let it stack up. Being free of debt gives you freedom. Learning to live without instant gratification is also good. I think that is another one of the big issues with people today. Not only do people want it today; they *have* to have it today. "Buy now and worry about it later" is a very dangerous philosophy. Not because of the one item you might have bought, but because it can become a slippery slope. What I hear most of all, including from myself occasionally, is "I *need* that." Not "want" but "need." Rarely do you actually need something. This simple change in vocabulary can put things back in the proper perspective.

I have been very fortunate in our finances, but it wasn't all luck. Here are a few rules that I use as a guide.

- Pay yourself first: Savings. Especially using your payroll deduction to make it easier. If you never actually get the money in your hands, it helps keep you disciplined.

- Always max out your employee savings plan, especially with any sort of company matching program.

- Always contribute the maximum on your 401(k) plan.

- Don't get greedy. "Pigs get feed, hogs get slaughtered." Remember that and remember that well. It has made me millions of dollars and helped me avoid making gargantuan mistakes. If you have a stock and you are up 30 percent on a big year, take some money off the table. Take the profit and re-diversify.

- Pay the church properly. Don't be one of those people, and there are so many, who continues to give what they did as a child. As an usher at my church, I see this all the time. Adults giving $5 or even $1. If they are in financial difficulties, that is completely different, and I am not talking about that at all. But, so many people just give so little. To be clear, even in our best financial years, we have never really committed to tithing up front in our annual pledge. I'm not proud to admit this; actually, it makes me somewhat ashamed. But, we have given a lot and are among the top financial supporters at our church. It is important to discuss the percentage or total amounts you want to contribute to charity or the church. We did often "tithe" with overall charitable giving and spread it out over many different charities.

- Company stock options. There are many different philosophies regarding stock options. The value of the option in itself is complicated. A mathematical model called Black-Scholes calculates it. There are many factors in the model to determine its value and I found examining each factor interesting. Notice I said interesting. It is valuable indeed but it didn't drive every decision. I don't think exercising options is complicated at all. Diversification is a key driver here. I think with all that has happened to Enron that I may have managed my personal risk better then the company experts managed their business. Choosing to exercise stock options isn't a commentary on your view of the company. I think it is fair to say that I "sipped the company Kool-Aid" as much as anyone but I still acted in a prudent conservative manner when it came to my family's future.

Remember, diversify your risk. There is nothing to argue about, just do it. Don't put all your money into your workplace. Remember, if your entire savings plan is going into your company stock, your retirement, your benefits, your options and don't forget your paycheck comes from there, diversify. No matter how bullish you are, be smart and diversify. Just do it. Even if you really believe, I mean really believe, remember there is event risk. What if your CEO dies in a plane wreck? What if your sector has a scandal? What if there has been a big accounting mistake and you have to restate earnings? Be disciplined. Here are a couple of real life examples that made millions of dollars of difference.

In May of 2001, we were buying a lot to build our dream house. We were moving to get Claire and Michael into the better individual schools within the Klein School District. Enron stock had dropped to $56 a share and we were all upset. It came time to close on the lot and I decided to pay cash for the lot and use Enron currency. I had made the decision earlier in the year that if we were to build our "dream" house, and spending a ton of money, I would use Enron currency to pay for it. I hate debt, especially big debt. Even though the stock had dropped to a price which I was convinced was a low price (I just knew the stock would come back to the $70s or higher), I remained disciplined to using Enron dollars to pay for the house. In fact, Chris was very upset with me for that decision. She really thought we were being shortsighted and giving up all of our upside. When I did exercise the options, just enough to cover the price of the lot, I was so frustrated; I threw down the phone in disgust. Little did we know that six months later Enron stock would be worthless and I would be unemployed! If

I had borrowed the money, I would have been unemployed and with $500,000 of additional debt! What a huge difference.

I have also always been disciplined about exercising options when they get deep in the money. Sometimes in the old days, they were barely in the money. I had many friends tell me that I was crazy and mathematically incorrect to exercise. They told me, "Don't sell the option, sell the optionality" or "Don't sell until it is late in the term; otherwise you are selling too cheaply and leaving money on the table." Yes, I sold options years before expiration but if an option is $30, $40 or $50 in the money, I say pull that money off the table and diversify. Many of my friends held, held and lost everything. They were "too clever by half." The lesson: Don't get greedy. The value of the option never contemplated that kind of hyper-value; therefore don't hesitate to take the money. Is this strategy always right? Of course not, but it is a conservative and sensible way to manage your money. Remember options are binary, they can be worth something or they can be worth nothing. This is especially true if you know you're are going to be reloaded or more options as you continue working. This is not to say that I did everything right. My net worth went down 75 percent with the downfall of Enron, but it could have been so much worse. Some of my friends and coworkers who didn't have a plan lost everything and will never forgive themselves. I may ask myself, "what ifs" but I am so fortunate, and I make it a priority to remember that.

The two hardest things to handle in life are failure and success.
—Unknown

Success is a process, not a status.
—Unknown

The world is full of things that couldn't possibly happen.
—Unknown

Success doesn't come to you, you go to it.
—Marva Collins

For success, try aspiration, inspiration and perspiration.
—Evan Esar

Nothing succeeds like the appearance of success.
—Christopher Lasch

It takes 20 years to make an overnight success.
—Eddie Cantor

Success is not measured by how you do compared to how somebody else does, but by how you do compared to what you could have done with what God gave you.
—Zig Ziglar

You can use most any measure when you're speaking of success. You can't measure it in a fancy home, expensive car or dress. But the measure of your real success is one you cannot spend—it's the way your child describes you when talking to a friend.
—Martin Buxbaum

Some people succeed because they are destined to succeed, but most people succeed because they are determined to succeed.
—Grant M. Bright

Success is the ability to go from one failure to another with no loss of enthusiasm.
—Sir Winston Churchill

Men are born to succeed, not to fail.
—Henry David Thoreau

Success is not a doorway; it's a stairway.
—Dottie Walters

SUCCESS

Success is as much the journey as it is the result. Also, everyone has his or her own measure of success. To some, being the second richest man in the world instead of the very top might be a huge failure. There are many examples of people who are barely getting by and who have nothing but their health and their children and yet feel very successful. It is as much a state of mind as anything else.

People actually fear success, down deep. You hear a lot about the fear of failure but the fear of success is closely related. There are also many examples of people who do stupid things and take themselves down without any apparent reason. There are also theories that a son has great difficulty being more successful than his father is. Whether it is guilt, or attitude or an invisible cap on oneself, I don't have a good answer for it but it seems to be real. When I first started being promoted, I began feeling this also. It wasn't obvious to me but I was very concerned and anxious and I didn't know why. Eventually, I realized that I was afraid of success. I had to work through this and it took a long time to be comfortable with it.

Success is up to you. Success is tied up with passion, dedication and your approach to life. You must strive at what you want and what you are doing. Success doesn't come to you; you go to it. People seem really to not understand any of this. Success is your life and how you measure it. It is neither absolute nor about everyone else's perspective. Remember the movie, *It's a Wonderful Life*? George Bailey was always more successful than his nemesis Mr. Potter. He simply didn't notice it. Certainly, Potter didn't notice it, nor did anyone else who was really paying attention. Why? Because it wasn't obvious and it wasn't up to them. It was up to George and his own measure of success and how he lived his life versus simply measuring success on the size of his bank account or how many cities he had visited. Internal reflection and achieving what you or your family really wants is the measure of success. If you haven't seen the movie for a while, stop and put it on your to-do list. Watch it often; it will never be a waste of time.

Each person has his own measure of success. I stated above that the second richest man in the world may consider himself a failure because he is number two. It's about expectations. Expectations should be high but the key is the subject or the focus. Should you focus on being the best dad in the world or the highest paid person in the department? Which one is nobler? I remember meeting Larry Ellison, the chairman and CEO of Oracle. The meeting may have been fun but it wasn't motivational. At the time, I was the CEO of Enron Technology, and Enron was a big customer of Oracle's. Larry came in to talk with my team, and I found him to be the most arrogant man I have ever met. He acted as if he honored us with his presence and just wanted to glorify how great he was and highlighted all of his celebrity friends and activities. What did he have to prove to us? Here we were talking to a very powerful and successful billionaire and top business executive, and he wanted to be sure that we were impressed with him. He also referred to Bill Gates in that conversation. I don't think Larry would be truly at peace until he was the richest person in the world—not just in the top five! A pretty high standard to keep! Needless to say, I never bought any Oracle stock.

The old computer-programming saying, "garbage in garbage out," applies in life and attitude, as well. Feed your mind the right mind food. If you fill it with negativism or bad or corrupting information, you are hurting yourself. Just like eating the right food for nutrition is important for your body, so is eating the right mental food for your brain. I really struggle with practicing this all the time. TV isn't very positive and I could watch TV all day. I have to be especially aware of the trap of watching trash TV or more risqué shows. I try to avoid it by turning the channel to something light or to The Learning Channel.

I learned something very interesting one fall. I was watching a great deal of trash type shows on TV. I decided to not watch any shows that were rated TV-14 or higher. Those shows included some of my favorites but they also included a lot of very suggestive behaviors and scenes. I also took this a step farther. I decided to substitute healthy and religious types of shows into the mix. What did I discover? It made a huge difference. I felt I had a better personality and healthier attitude.

Lay out a personal definition of success, think about it and then go for it. People often don't notice what activities bring them success. They focus on what they don't have versus what they do have. Appreciating what you have is a section in this book and could be an entire book it itself. The world is full of examples of success and it is very important to study them. You will learn things—big or small—about why someone made it or what drove him or her to success. In fact, you may also learn things about yourself and what will drive you to success.

Bad things happen; put your past behind you.
—*The Lion King*

Use failure as fertilizer.
—Denis Waitley

Failure is delay, not defeat.
—Denis Waitley

Failure is our teacher, not our undertaker.
—Denis Waitley

There is no failure except in no longer trying.
—Elbert Hubbard

Believe you are defeated, believe it long enough, and it is likely to
become a fact.
—Norman Vincent Peale

Failure is not fatal, but failure to change might be.
—John Wooden

You learn from successful failures.
—Glenn Ebersole

Failure is a detour, not a dead-end street.
—Zig Ziglar

Our greatest glory consists not in never failing, but in rising every time
we fall.
—Oliver Goldsmith

Failure, rejection and mistakes are the perfect stepping-stones to success.
—Dale Carnegie

You always pass failure on the way to success.
—Mickey Rooney

What would you do if you weren't afraid?
—Spencer Johnson

A stumble may prevent a fall.
—English Proverb

Success is not forever and failure isn't fatal.
—Don Shula

FAILURE

Fear of failure has to be one of the greatest negative influences on people in business or in general. Failure can freeze some people, mentally or physically. I think they absolutely believe that failure is their destroyer or will take them down. They don't view it as feedback.

Fear of failure is very similar to fear of success. If a person really looked and internalized what a particular failure would mean, I think it would help them make decisions. Some failures are so minor or have such minor consequences, that the decision should be to go for it. Often, the real failure is in neglecting to examine the problem correctly. I read an example that helps me keep things in perspective. I think it was in *The Power of Positive Thinking* by Dr. Norman Vincent Peale. In golf, hitting a ball from the rough can cause people to make a mistake by over-thinking or worrying about the shot. If you break down the problem a little further, the golf ball is merely sitting in thicker grass, which is not actually very dense or overly difficult. Go down and really look at the ball. Pick the grass around it; it is actually just little blades of grass with a great deal of air around the grass. Pick some of it and eat it. There is nothing to it. Why should you over-think a golf shot from the rough? Life is like this analogy. Quite often, if you break down the problem or situation, the risks are not that great; the obstacles not so huge, the worst-case result not significant … go for it.

Taking on failure and not letting it get you down and actually learning from it is obviously much easier said than done. If you can get over the crippling effect failure often has on people, you have an enormous advantage in business and life itself. It will take you in new directions and in areas many people wouldn't dare to go. I often grapple with confidence issues, but everything I have done and every success I have tells me that I should be confident. I learned a very valuable lesson about this from an unexpected source. When Jeff Shankman and I started up Enron Global Markets (EGM), he made a comment that I will not soon forget. We were talking about our different backgrounds and personalities when he said something that really hit me. He told me that he could work for me with no problems and that I was better suited for the top job. I didn't really believe his view, of course, but his explanation was fascinating. He stated that he was a great trader and proud of his accomplishments, but that was all he knew how to do. He said that he didn't substantially change jobs because he was scared to. I, on the other hand, had done many things and proven my abilities in many areas of business and I was the best candidate to be the CEO. I almost fell over; even if I doubted his sincerity, his message was fascinating. I guess I needed to review my background more and realize that I really can do many things and that I can handle or at least put failure in context.

Real failure is not listening to or learning from the failed event. Having persistence doesn't mean you do something that didn't work repeatedly. It means learning from each attempt and adjusting your thinking and using failure as feedback.

Remember that every success or failure, no matter how small, teaches you and takes you in new direction. Even a very small change or thought direction. Just think about how great life would be if you approached every situation or problem without any fear of failure. Think about what you could achieve without holding yourself back. Imagine a world with everyone doing that. Just imagine a world like that and the types of opportunities you would have in it. I really want you to ponder this. Stop and think about some situation where you didn't go for it. Think about why. Certainly, there are very good reasons why you shouldn't do some things, but make sure you have a reason. Make it a choice not due to fear. Imagine if you weren't afraid. What could you have done? It may even drive you to write a book to help your kids or other people to have a better life.

Fear of failure does have big effects on people. We should take a lesson from professional baseball players. The very best of pro ball players have a batting average of .300. That is 3 out of 10. 30 percent, are you kidding me? A star hits 30 percent of the time he is at the plate? That is an "F" is school, actually an F-. It is a good lesson. They strike out all the time but have to deal with it and step right back up and take another swing. We have a tendency to remember every failure no matter how small and punish ourselves with that failure. We should think more like a baseball star. Remember the greatest of them all, Babe Ruth, struck out 10,000 times.

The person who has no imagination has no wings.
—Muhammad Ali

You need to see yourself as already being and achieving your objective.
—Unknown

Visualize, prayerize, actionize and your wishes will come true.
—Charles L. Allen

Vision is having an acute sense of the possible. It is seeing what others don't see. And when those with similar vision are drawn together, something extraordinary happens.
—Unknown

Imagination is the eye of the soul.
—Joseph Joubert

Change your thoughts and you change the world.
—Norman Vincent Peale

Most people see what is and never see what can be.
—Unknown

Where there is no vision, the people perish.
—Proverbs 19:18

Close your eyes and visualize the person you really want to be, who fits your own concept of self-respect. If you can see the person clearly in the mirror of your mind, you surely will become that person.
—Denis Waitley

The best way to predict your future is to create it.
—Unknown

If you have built castles in the air, your work need not be lost; that is where they should be. Now, put foundations under them.
—Henry David Thoreau

Nothing happens unless first a dream.
—Carl Sandburg

Our aspirations are our possibilities.
—Robert Browning

VISIONING

Professional athletes use visioning and give it the highest of credits for their success. The same applies to life and to business. I certainly do it, although not always. I also find that the times I don't do it, I don't perform as well or simply can't seem to reach the goal as consistently as I should.

The proper visioning is important too. If you want to vision making a putt on the golf course, you don't say to yourself, "Don't leave it short," or you will do just that. Your mind is like a magnet. It will attract what you think. If you said to yourself not to do something, your natural tendency will be to do the very thing that you said or thought. You should practice visioning and setting positive expectations. Always, **always,** state things in the positive. When I putt, I think about leaving it 8 inches long. Dr. Denis Waitley talked about this in his very insightful book, *The Psychology of Winning*. This concept and his example of pitching, which is along the same line as the putting example, is something I have never forgotten. There was a home run hitter up to bat with the pitcher thinking about how the batter preferred inside pitches. He thought, "Don't throw it inside." He then threw it inside and the batter hit another home run. The pitcher should have repeated to himself, throw it outside. Don't say the negative; state the objective in the positive.

Also, if you really think about it, if you really focus on it and mentally practice or have the vision, you've already done it. If you focus hard enough and in a proper realistic deep fashion, your body can't tell the difference. Your mind really doesn't know that you haven't done it all before. The returning prisoners of war from Vietnam proved that. There are examples of prisoners that played a pretend guitar every day for years and didn't lose a step when they returned and played it for real. In addition, people actually learned how to play well without a real guitar; they learned and practiced in their minds. There was another example of a POW who returned home and played in a pro-am golf tournament in New Orleans a week after coming back home. He shot in the 70s after not playing for 7 years. Actually, he had played every, single day for all those years—in his mind. He had done it mentally; and done it perfectly.

Remember the very first time you drove the car on your own after you got your drivers license? Just like how driving got easier every time you got behind the wheel of a car, every time you visualize a successful outcome, whatever it is, you'll be better at it. I have given a lot of presentations and speeches. In preparing for them, I practice many times. I also practice and imagine the reaction of the crowd. I do it enough times that, even if I had a stack of notes, I don't really need to do anything but glance at them. Why? I already delivered the actual speech many times.

The more you do this, the better result you will achieve. Once you think about this concept, you will notice two things. First, you will find it works. Second, you will realize how often you hear things expressed in the negative and then how often that result is what actually happens. It is as if you know a secret that no one else knows. It's funny but it really helps.

Chapter Six:

Empowerment

Success is all in the mind.
—Robin Daubeny

One thing that has had a profound effect on my life is an odd item, at first glance. I discovered this while reading the book, *Unlimited Power* by Anthony Robbins. In his book, he addressed the fact that your mind is always on, especially subliminally. His point was this: Why do you suddenly remember where your lost keys are while in the shower or doing something totally unrelated? His view was that a person who lost his keys was actually constantly thinking about where those keys were. They asked themselves an open-ended question when they originally realized they had lost them. With that open-ended question, your mind keeps searching.

Robbins then goes on to use this concept and change it. He asked, "What if you were to focus your mind on positive thoughts?" So many people ask themselves open-ended negative questions. Questions like, "Why do I have to go to work today? Why can't I sleep in? Why can't it be Saturday?" Robbins stated, just imagine if you asked yourself positive or empowering questions. Interesting thought, I remember thinking. I believe so much of the power of belief and attitude so this made a lot of sense to me. He suggested you try to ask yourself three empowering questions and see what happens. In 1993, what did happen was significant. In fact, the effects were very visible and noticeable. I always asked myself three questions in the morning: What can I do today to make Chris and Claire feel happy and loved? What can I do today to bring us closer to God? What can I do today to solve the FP&L deal? What I found was very interesting, actually stunning. Without actually thinking about it directly, I found that we started going to church and I prayed more regularly. I found myself buying flowers and calling Chris in the middle of the day. I did this so often that she called me on it and asked me why I was calling her so much. In addition, a huge event happened. After a few weeks of my morning ritual, Geoff Roberts and I were on a plane going to a meeting with FP&L for our ongoing negotiations when suddenly it hit me. The solution that changed the course of the negotiations came out of the blue. We were several months into a termination provision but we didn't have very much leverage in the negotiations and were up against people who were difficult to deal with. They felt they had all the cards and that was their overall corporate persona. While on that trip with Geoff, I discovered a new twist on our ongoing supply obligation in the contract. I jumped out of my seat, in the coach section, and ran up to tell Geoff (in first class) my good news. After getting a dirty look from the flight attendant for entering first class, I eagerly touched him on the shoulder and said that I found the answer. It proved to be so and over the next two months, we signed a new agreement that saved the company $451 million dollars (NPV). It also earned me my first significant bonus and a big promotion. A few months later, we were off to London in 1994 for my next job and one that also led to many significant promotions.

It happened to me again in London. I was a vice president in charge of renegotiating a devastating contract, in which the prices were more than $2.3 billion above the current market price. It was the biggest problem and project in the company. I was on a double-decker bus going to work when literally the same thing happened: The answer popped right into my head, just as it had on the plane, and I ran to work. I called Jeff Skilling and it was the beginning of the solution.

I realize that this sounds a bit of an odd concept but try it. Of all the exercises I have done, this has had the most profound impact on my life. In fact, when I am really "in the zone" with this, I will put my three empowering questions on my mirror, so I will see them every morning. It works wonders, and makes me ask myself why I don't use this technique more often. It has solved many problems and really changed my life.

POSITIVE SELF-TALK

Your mind pays attention and records everything you say.

Your mind pays attention and records everything you say. I mean everything, whether it is silently or aloud. Even if you don't agree, imagine that this is true for a moment. As an example, if you call yourself stupid or dumb once a day for a year, you've told yourself that 365 times. You don't think that makes an impact on you? Try calling a child that 365 time and watch what happens.

This brings to mind an example I am ashamed to reference, but I think I should. Never use negative criticism, especially with a child. Never violate this rule, no matter how mad or frustrated you are. I occasionally would be furious with my son and would slip and call him a name. He would do something that I found ridiculous, and I would lose control and yell, "Don't be stupid!" or "Don't be a moron!" He would run out of the room absolutely crushed. I would go talk to him and feel awful. I hated it when I did that. If I play it back in my mind, it sounds so awful and nasty. Calling my child a name? Nice. It embarrasses me greatly, admitting this in writing.

If we accept that directing negative criticism at someone else affects how that person feels about himself or herself, why, then, do we find it so hard to believe self-directed negativity will have the same result? I admit that I have found practicing positive self-talk is very difficult to do, but I constantly try to improve in this area. When I get mad at myself or angry at something and call myself something negative, I really do think it has a negative impact. It is simply a logical conclusion. Try changing your behavior right now and stop being self-defeating. I will keep working on this, as well.

TAKE COMMAND

Tomorrow is now.
—Eleanor Roosevelt

This was another of General Schwarzkopf's key leadership points. When in command, take command. This is a matter of responsibility and accountability. I think people really like having an escape mechanism from accountability. If you have been put in command, you must take command and do the job. Just do it. At work, that is what is expected and why the company put you in charge. It may not be fun or the kind of thing that lives up to its cool sounding nature. It is lonely and difficult and something that many people simply can't do. Too often, people believe that if they don't take command, they are not responsible or accountable. If things go badly or negatively, it wasn't their fault, it happened to them. This is total nonsense. It is one of the biggest and most serious issues in today's society. So many people skirt or really believe they aren't in control or accountable for their lives or actions. It is total BS. If you are successful, you did it and you are responsible. If you fail, you did it and you are responsible. Feeling any other way is unacceptable and makes you a weak person. That certainly doesn't mean you succeed or fail strictly by your actions alone. I am not trying to say that teamwork and co-workers aren't important. I'm talking here about responsibility and accountability, not taking credit or increasing your self-importance. Circumstances, luck, uncontrollable events all influence life and success but even with those factors, your choices on how you act or react to them is your responsibility. You are in command.

Chapter Seven:

Knowledge

You can always learn. In fact, if you're not learning, you're dying. At the very least, you are moving backwards and a part of you does die each day. Plus, what a wasted opportunity. Every day presents a new opportunity. It is very important to find something you are interested in and pursue it. Every movie you watch, every book you read, every conversation you have presents an opportunity to learn and grow. You don't have to take a lot away from a particular event. All things build on each other and make a new you, or at least turn you in a slightly new direction or nudge you to become a slightly new individual. Each thing or event makes you learn or absorb something new and it changes you, even in the slightest of ways. And, you can watch the same show or documentary repeatedly and you will see or feel different ways depending on your mood or thoughts at that moment in time. Each event will affect you even in the slightest of ways.

Make learning happen. Take a class, listen to famous speeches, attend lectures, read books, watch more educational TV, rent videos. Shake things up. It will help you grow and change as a person. This doesn't mean only do things to improve yourself. Learning more about things outside work or your normal life also improves you. If you focus on good and positive learning events, it will make a real difference. In fact the old saying "garbage in, garbage out" is accurate. It is just like watching trash on TV. It teaches you something; it's just negative or a darker side of life. You don't need it. It doesn't help you and actually takes you backward. I wish I could say that I practice this religiously but sometimes I slip as well.

Once when I was sick and in bed, I watched a documentary on WWII. This actually became a habit whenever I got sick, which is too often due to my diabetes. I think each time I watched it I was more appreciative of life, sacrifice, commitment, freedom and being an American. It made me very appreciative and thankful for our lives and for what we have as a family.

My TV habit is so strong. I do find ways to take advantage of it and turn it into a positive, however. Well, at least sometimes.

I love to learn. I constantly buy or hope to get for Christmas all different kinds of reference books; books on space, history, old atlases, photo essays of the 20th Century, art, the American presidency, English kings and queens and so many others. I have so much yet to learn, and I consider that a gift, in itself.

MY FRATERNITY, SIGMA PHI EPSILON

I got a tremendous education at the University of Oklahoma. I had some great professors including adjunct professors who were experts in the industry. The petroleum land management degree was the best in the country. When people think of great schools, OU rarely comes to mind. However, it is very true for some majors like geology, petroleum engineering and petroleum land management. I am proud of my degree and school and that doesn't even count my love for Sooner football.

One activity that shaped me more than I could ever dream at the time was joining a fraternity, Sigma Phi Epsilon (Sig Ep for short). Academic knowledge is important, of course, but the social skills and the ability to interact with people has stayed with me much longer than remembering a particular math formula or identifying a rock type. I grew so much in my fraternity, and I use the skills developed there on a daily basis. Contacts, as well, should never be overlooked or underestimated. If there is any doubt on whether to join a fraternity/sorority or remain independent, join the group. On many campuses, especially at OU, it was a very strong group and one that provided such a great platform for fun, sports and of course studying. It is not just a party but you develop discipline and friendships that will stay with you forever.

Each fraternity or sorority has its own personality. I joined Sig Ep but my best friend and college roommate, Pete Brzycki, joined Delta Upsilon (DU). That fraternity fit his personality better and he had the guts to step out and join it. Actually, he is one of the reasons I added this section. Pete was my best friend in high school and was my freshman college roommate. He is a great person and had a significant influence on my life. I witnessed firsthand the positive effects of these organizations had on both Pete and my sister Anne. The encouragement and acceptance as part of a large group developed social and leadership skills that would have remained below the surface of their personalities—maybe forever. If anyone asks you for advice on this, please don't just encourage, but push him or her in this direction.

BOOKS ON TAPE

A book is like a garden carried in your pocket.

As I got older, or simply worked harder and harder, I found less and less time for reading. I think reading and expanding your mind is so important. Except for vacations, I had stopped reading books for enjoyment all together. While working for Excel Resources in the early 1990s, I discovered books on tape. I was able to get exposure to books or ideas I would never have had time to read, by listening to different novels or authors in the car commuting to work. For quite some time I focused on positive thinking or motivational types of books, but that expanded quite significantly. Over the years I've read, actually listened to, hundreds of books. This collection includes about every type of book that exists.

I find that my taste or choices vary a great deal. As I have stated many times I believe that you may choose what you need or are in the mood for. "When the student is ready, the teacher student will come." My book selection moves from fiction to non-fiction, business to physics, abridged to non-abridged. I both buy and rent various books. For years, I had a great and easy system. Randalls grocery store rented books on tape for $1.00 for three days. What a deal. I must have rented more than 100 titles from Randalls. I pretty much ran out of books to hear. Then suddenly, Randalls got out of the video/audio rental business and I was in trouble. I bought several books but that got really expensive really fast. A book on tape cost just as much as a book in hard cover. Then I discovered the Houston Public Library. For a long time they didn't have a very good selection of books on tape, but that changed over the years. Now they have a significant selection, arranged by category. When I finish a book, I often go into the library without a specific book in mind and see how the spirit moves me. As an example of my eclectic tastes, I have recently gone from listening to the first two books by Jean Auel, the *Clan of the Cave Bear* and *The Valley of Horses* to *Star Wars* to *The Vicar* by Agatha Christi to Ayn Rand's *Anthem* to Stephen Hawkins *A Brief History of Time*. That is some variety and all in a three-month period. I'm not sure what that says about my attention span or me, but I do like to have variety. I also live by an expression: A mind is like a rubber band; once stretched, it can't go back to its original shape.

I also really liked changing the paradigm. I turned a very negative part of my life, a long daily commute downtown, into one that I actually anticipated. In fact there were many times that I would be parked in the parking garage at work and would stay out in the car waiting for the chapter to end. I like solving problems that way.

I am extremely well read. Well, well listened. Try this for yourself.

Section 2—Management and Business Approaches

Chapter One:

Values

Your company will have a set of rules or guidelines it believes in. It will have a set of principles and a mission. Don't dismiss this. Many people and employees will downplay this as part of the company. I recommend you pay attention to this. Do the senior players believe in what is out there? Do they downplay or make fun of this part of the company? On these "softer" management issues there are various reactions. If you simply cram these issues down to the employees, they will be very skeptical and believe they are just words. Ken Lay recognized that Enron was slipping in its commitment to values and he formed a Vision and Values committee to correct the problem. Once the values were in place, we made sure to connect them with actions and recognize people who walk the talk on the values. It was an interesting process. Ken Lay was the chief promoter. He thought it was vital to live by these rules and to be a company of principle. In the aftermath of the meltdown, it appears very hypocritical but I know that we really believed in them. Our president and COO was a different story. To get him interested at all, we had to tie it constantly to earnings or how the employees would be more productive, thus translating it into more profit. I remember clearly a strategy to get him to back these. I had to go with the chair of the committee, a woman he didn't respect or take seriously at all, and make a presentation on the importance of our values to increased profitability. When I think back on those events, it makes me feel foolish. Why should we have to convince the president that living by values like these was a no-brainer? It was like not being for America or apple pie. I should have paid attention to the difficulty of this and at the very least, it should have raised a red flag that his moral compass was a mess. There were many others who thought it was stupid and a waste of time. I thought it was their youth and immaturity, but it was much more. They weren't living up to their own values. Actually, they probably didn't have any values at all. Some of these people were very senior and leaders of large organizations. We had a culture that was out of control and I didn't recognize its seriousness.

If you agree with the stated priorities and corporate principles, live by them. It will make you a better employee and reinforce whether you want to be with the company. At Enron, if we had held fast to our four values of respect, integrity, communication and excellence, we would still be a strong, innovative company today. I was a founding member of the Vision and Values Committee and our goal was to indoctrinate those values and get everyone excited about living those principles at work. And, I would do it again today.

VISION

Where there is not vision, the people perish.

You must have a vision. If you are in a position of leadership, your vision may be the reason why. You must not only have the vision but also set it and get everyone to buy into it. If you know you are right and you have the support of your boss, then you must implement what you believe. Think it through carefully, and ensure you have buy-in. It doesn't have to be only your vision. In fact, if it has everyone's signature on it, it will certainly be more successful. I believe that setting the vision and having the group fully develop it is much better. If you are gaining momentum with your vision, and you know you are doing the right thing, then your key people must buy in. If they don't then it will fail.

Vision relates to setting corporate goals and objectives, but I thought it deserved a separate mention. Your vision sets the pace and creates action steps toward the future. The more I contemplate all my work experience, the more I see clearly who really had vision versus the ability to drive for results. It is a special person, a real leader who can do both. It is something very clear about people who make good chief executive officers versus those who make good chief operating officers. Many cannot make the transition when faced with the opportunity. A successful CEO is much more than a promoted, successful or smart person. At Enron, we were very long on IQ (actually it is amazing how many smart people were at the company), but we often promoted these brilliant people into significant leadership positions rather than paying them extremely well and leaving them where they were world-class in their fields. They lacked vision. I can name a dozen management mistakes that produced very bad and counter-productive results. Vision is a key here. Being at the top of your field versus having vision and the ability to lead a large number of employees are often very different.

Never underestimate the importance of vision and the profound, positive effect it can have on your ability to achieve.

BALANCE

Think about your priorities.

This is one of the most difficult issues to tackle. I think about it all the time but do not do a good job of practicing what I preach. I am convinced that without proper balance, life begins to unravel. It shows itself in many different ways and each reminds you of the importance of balance. It may appear as lack of sleep, excessive worry, arguments with your wife or your kids not talking with you, but it will show up. I have found that wives are very good at raising the issue. Nagging is a better word for it. The problem is that if they don't nag at you, then you get worse and really get out of balance. This is one of the biggest challenges any worker will face. I saw an excellent example many years ago that I wish I had kept. It was a graphic that compared a person's life to a wheel. When a wheel gets out of balance on your car, damage will occur. First it will be the tire itself but then it can lead to alignment problems or much worse. I believe your life is similar to that.

There was a time in my life when I really lost my balance. A major struggle exists between working hard everyday and staying focused on family. My daughter Claire taught me this lesson in a very disturbing and even shameful way. When I was CEO of Global Markets, my schedule was so crazy I would work myself to exhaustion. Finally, the inevitable happened. We were at the dinner table one evening, and it was my turn to inform everyone what I was going to give up for Lent. I couldn't think of anything and Claire piped up with a suggestion. "I know what you can give up Daddy," she said. "What is that sweetheart?" I replied. "You can give up falling asleep at the dinner table." Writing this even now, years later, puts a pit in my stomach. Be careful that a work ethic doesn't turn into something harmful.

This is definitely a work in progress. At the very least, I want you to think about it and pay attention to it. I certainly wish I had been more proactive here but thank goodness, it didn't have any long-term consequences. If you don't listen or see your possible balance issues, you may not be so lucky.

BEING GROUNDED

You must think about what is really important.

As success continues and work is going well, your perspective can change very quickly. You don't actually see it but gradually you begin to change and become more demanding and impatient. I have noticed and been reminded of this by Chris many times. In the world of two secretaries, private jets, meetings that wait on you to begin, it is so easy to let it affect you and to become a true elitist. That in turn changes you as a person. Your expectations begin to change and you find yourself saying things that aren't very nice and are very harsh. Usually I don't actually say them but sadly, I often think them as I go through the day. I must fight this battle constantly. If you let your guard down, it gets out of control very quickly. Feelings of importance turn into feelings of superiority that become very real, and the belief that you should get better treatment becomes commonplace. The idea that you shouldn't have to wait in line or that other people should always make allowances for your position or very busy schedule become simply expected. As I write this, I am particularly ashamed. I did have some of these feelings and I have prayed a lot for forgiveness. Just because I was one of the better ones about this in my peer group, doesn't give me solace.

Think about this a lot. I do believe that you make your own luck, but your good fortune doesn't make you better than someone else. You should actually be more patient, because of just how blessed you have been. When you think about just how "special" you are and how you shouldn't have to put up with a line at a department store, think about what Jesus would think. Stop and think about that. You should be ashamed just by reading this. I know that I am. Jesus, the savior of the world, was born in a stable and was raised in a very poor environment. Would you have looked down upon him because of that? Maybe next time you are feeling so good about yourself, you should stop and let the other person go ahead of you.

If you want to evaluate yourself, just listen to yourself. When you make a statement aloud or in your mind, think about exactly what you just said. Playing that back in your mind will be a wake-up call. Think about people who are really struggling to get though every day and just how lucky you really are.

BASIC PRINCIPLES

Integrity is everything.

You can't compromise this ever. First, you need to know what your principles are. What do you stand for? Whenever you compromise these, you will suffer and there will be a price. After all the difficulties I experienced with the downfall of Enron, I realized many people got in trouble because they waived their own principles and foundation. You can't let a crack enter your foundation. Not a single crack. Warren Buffet, one of the giants in business for the 20th Century, lives by a saying that I believe is very true. He said, "You shouldn't do anything you would be afraid would show up on the front page of the paper." Not a bad standard to live by.

If you ever don't know what to do, you could always turn to the Ten Commandments. What are your standards and principles? This book lists some of mine. You should have one, too. Start a list; write down your own code of conduct. Once you identify your principles in writing, it will be easy to live by your code. Don't forget to be very specific.

Now that you have identified your basic principles, you must never breach them. This includes small breaches that no one would ever know or hear about. If you are not sure what your basic principles are, write them down and force yourself to look at them and think them through. An honest person is one who sticks by his or her principles even if the consequences can be costly. I can assure you that issues and dilemmas will appear and test you. Although at that time, it will be a huge call or a huge action that could have enormous consequences; you still must follow your principles. It may cost you at the time—possibly a severe consequence. If you give in and do something or look the other way, there will be a cost as well. In fact, it will most certainly be worse, just at a later date. It may be personal and one that may cause many sleepless nights.

I have had to lay off or fire people. These are very difficult things to do, but if you treat people with respect, if you do it with integrity and for the right reasons, you have given them the proper chances, and they have made bad choices, you can do it with a clear conscience.

I want to clarify a point. Executing corporate decisions that you may not agree with is very different from a violation of your principles. Remember, your boss is still the boss and he may be accountable for the future of the company or department. If someone is telling you to do something that is wrong, you should always do what is right. You don't need to quit necessarily, depending on what the issue is, but you should look for a new job and go somewhere that will not compromised your ethics. Disagreeing with a corporate strategy or direction is an entirely different area.

Chapter Two:

People

BELIEVE IN PEOPLE

Most people don't have any idea how great they can be.

Believe that people can do their jobs and give them the benefit of the doubt. That doesn't mean you let them go on forever if they aren't doing well or have a troubled past, but you should give them a chance. When you give them a real review of their skills and a thorough assessment, if they aren't cutting it, you must take action. You should never go into the review period or trial with a biased view. There are exceptions to this when you take over a new job or responsibility but if a person is trying and has a good or right kind of attitude, they have a fresh start with me. If you need input, get it. Get third-party feedback and cross calibrate. This will get you a new opinion that isn't influenced by any personal feelings. In addition, you can learn what skills or attributes are real strengths of the person. In London, I had a peer, then employee, who was struggling in one job. He had incredible language and diplomatic skills that he developed in his law school training at Oxford. I thought he would be a great regulatory person and we transferred him into a new position. He wasn't happy about it at first but he was great at it and eventually opened a new office in Brussels and was very successful. Help people succeed.

Some very smart people managed big groups at Enron and some of them would come into every job with the attitude that an employee is lacking or incompetent until he proves otherwise. Wrong idea, very wrong idea. I believe there are cases in which a department or function is not working and may need a significant change but I always approach it with the belief that the people have value and under new management or philosophy may do very well. They will also appreciate it. I would much prefer to believe in people's abilities than to make them prove themselves repeatedly.

Believing in people can really test your faith sometimes, but you must always do what you know is right. Remember my friend Kevin Howard, from the "Prayer Power" chapter? Unfortunately, his story has a bad postscript. Incredibly, the Department of Justice decided to try Kevin Howard and Mike Krautz again. Although they had not been able to get a single guilty verdict in the first trial, they were off trying again. The prosecution changed its strategy and made the case more about character and the so-called "bad" people of Enron, rather than an illegal transaction. I testified in the trial. I felt compelled to do so. It was a very scary thing to do. I had spent five years off the radar screen of the entire process, but I was going to intentionally walk back in and put some focus on me. I lost a lot of sleep over this decision, but I knew I was doing the right thing.

After several days of being on call to testify, the day finally arrived to go down and do it. Chris and I arrived at noon for a 1:30 start time as was requested by Kevin's lawyer. The case was still moving very slowly, and we had to wait for several hours in a small conference room before finally going in at 4 p.m. Just before we entered the little waiting room for the court, Ken Lay and Jeff Skilling walked by as they returned from lunch to their trial, which was right next door! It was nice talking with both of them, and they actually looked good. I can't imagine what they were going through. Five months of being on trial and portrayed by the media as someone as evil as the Antichrist must have been so hard on them, but you couldn't a seen it on their faces. After a quick conversation with all in their family, they both thanked me for testifying for Kevin because they were angry that he had been dragged into this mess. After this, I was in the waiting room for several more hours. I was worried that we were going to be put off another day (a day I couldn't afford because I had to be in Austin the next morning), but soon, we were on. I wasn't on the stand very long and was able to make the points I really wanted to make. It certainly wasn't easy to do, though. The prosecutor interrupted me at every question, literally. He was extremely arrogant, and the judge actually overruled him every time. I learned just how ugly the process actually is. It's not about justice at all but about winning at any cost. In fact, as I was waiting my turn on the witness stand, two FBI agents approached me and acted as if we were old friends. They actually offered me advice! I saw this for what it was—an attempt to get inside my head and make me believe they were watching me.

I was in Austin on May 30 when Kevin Howard's verdict came in, and he was convicted on all five counts. Earlier in the year he got a hung jury and thus was "not guilty" on 20 counts. Mike Krautz, the accountant with him, was acquitted; thank God for that. I didn't know him very well, but everyone liked him and believed he was a tragic victim of the witch-hunt. Kevin is a wonderful man and faced going to jail for most of the rest of his life. This was is a travesty, a total travesty. This shouldn't happen in America. Juries should not be able to make such a big mistake. They shouldn't put someone in jail because he made some money and used to work at Enron. Chris then reminded me that juries are just people and that 60 million people watch *American Idol*. There are more votes cast for a reality show contestant than for President of the United States. My initial reaction was that it's difficult to be proud to be an American under these circumstances. It just isn't right.

The e-mails had begun. Terry, Kevin's assistant, and my old assistant Cathy were crying while typing what they were feeling and thinking. I sent Kevin an e-mail, telling him how sorry I was and, incredibly, I got an e-mail back from him. He consoled me and told me to hang in there and to keep the faith in God! He consoled me? I am not sure if I was more shocked by his incredible faith or by the fact that he was worried about me! Two weeks later, I had lunch with Kevin and another mutual friend, Greg Sharp. Again, Kevin emphasized to keep faith in God and this was part of his plan; we just didn't understand his long-term plan. How could he feel that way? The decision devastated me, but the person who was going to jail was at peace with it, at least for the moment.

Kevin told me he planned to file an appeal, but there was a major problem: he had no money and was deep in debt. The trial had wiped him out and he was on the verge of being unable to pay his bills or even keep his family in their house—never mind paying another appellate lawyer. As Kevin dealt with these realities, the first of two miracles happened. Jeff McMahon, about whom I have written several times already, started a fund for people to contribute money to help Kevin and his family. The fund was set up to allow up to $10,000 per individual contribution. The donations came pouring in. Each time I received an update from Jeff, I would actually giggle aloud, so many people were stepping up. Chris and I contributed, as well, after some serious discussions about how much we could give. It was the biggest single donation we had ever made, outside of church. It meant we would not take a vacation this year, among other cutbacks, but it was the right thing to do. The kids understood as best they could, but I know it was difficult for them. And, we soon found out we were not the only ones to stretch our limits: the fund ultimately surpassed $240,000. Think about that. People contributed $240,000 to help a man who had been convicted of a felony. What an inspirational life lesson and testament to the character of Kevin.

Thank God for Jeff and his commitment and for everyone else who stepped up to help. Kevin was able to hire the right appellate lawyer, who actually cut his fee in half because he believed the conviction was a travesty of justice. The positive energy generated by the success of the fund was interrupted, unfortunately. Over the summer, Kevin's mother died. How emotionally devastated can one person be? How much grief can one person be expected to deal with? Kevin's incredible nature allowed him to see even this as a blessing, providing more inspiration for the rest of us from one man's life.

On the legal front, good news was developing. Kevin's appeal had gained momentum and the prosecution supported a sentencing delay. This was a positive sign about the outcome of his appeal, and it would get even better. The judge vacated all of the five convictions. Dropped convictions! That simply does not happen. All that we had said and believed about the guilty verdicts having been a travesty was bearing out. All our prayers for real justice were paying off. I hope this nightmare is close to being over for such a wonderful man and his family.

It is very important to be quietly ready to help someone who is struggling in smaller ways, too. If someone is presenting an idea and is tongue-tied or nervous, your insertion of a comment or can help him or her regroup. If you are doing it for the right reason, it is a great feeling. If you jump in and take the spotlight away from the person, you are hurting that person and taking away a small piece of confidence. Lending a hand is something you don't have to discuss; people know if someone has helped them. They will pass this on later and help someone else. Office politics can be ruthless, but you can't let someone get hurt because they are nervous. It is another matter entirely if a person fails because he or she wasn't prepared or lied or for some other devious reason. However, you should help someone when he or she needs it. Jumping in and adding a comment allows them to take a breath and regain composure. If you've had good bosses, they have done it for you, too.

CARE ABOUT PEOPLE

People know when you care about them. I certainly don't mean to fake any feelings or views but if you have passion about something and really care about it, people will know. Of course, when you don't, people know that, too. If you really don't care about a group or a person, maybe you shouldn't be doing that job. A good manager has to deal with the conflict between what is good for the person or his feelings for that individual and what is best for the business. It is a difficult thing to balance. By caring about people, I don't mean you have to cod-dle them or treat them with great emotion. It means you should respect them as individuals and consider their lives when thinking about taking an action. It means being honest with them and keeping them informed. It means giving them chances when they deserve chances. And, if you must terminate them, it means they have had honest feedback and they chose not to change or to you're your feedback.

I can't tell you how many big decisions were made by leaders in the company during difficult times where they talked about individuals as if they were cattle or simply numbers on a fact sheet. It is inexcusable. Caring about people doesn't mean you're soft or weak. People often misinterpret niceness as weakness. It actu-ally means you're strong and that you live by principles. Some people never understand that. Living in a business world that can be harsh and full of people like that is your challenge. Notice I said challenge, not downfall. If it is your downfall, you should have left already. Alternatively, upon realizing that your views would not be accepted, you should have been looking for a new job in a new company. People who were harsh and self-serving surrounded me. My meth-ods and thought processes weren't the norm but the people I cared about cer-tainly didn't look down upon them. You must do the right thing for the business and shareholders but the approach does make a difference and it produces a bet-ter result.

BE GENUINE AND OPEN WITH PEOPLE

I have always been a very open person, actually an open book. Again, much more so than I probably should have been at times. If you have a lighter side, don't hide it. Everyone around me knows me pretty well and that includes my goofy side. I laugh alone and think funny things and yes, I get a kick out of dumb things—sometimes, the sillier the better. Not your normal CEO personality or appearance. I think the upside though is also very positive. People know where I stand and there aren't surprises. People can count on that, feel at ease with deci-sions, and have the confidence to move forward feeling empowered and account-able. This will pay off in the end. With the entire collapse of Enron, most people are very mad at the senior management of the company. Of all the senior people, I think employees have given me the benefit of the doubt more than anyone else has. That certainly makes me sleep better at night. Part of being genuine and open is simple communication. It also relates to respect.

TREAT PEOPLE WITH RESPECT, AT ALL LEVELS

You can learn a lot about a person by the way he treats the people under him. It gets to the core of a person. As I became more successful and my time became more and more valuable, it really affected me. I had designed everything at work to save me time or make my life easier so that I could focus my efforts on important things and be free from distraction. Living in a world of corporate planes, multiple assistants and limos makes you start to believe that you actually a better person or more important than others. That translates into action and not treating people with the respect they deserve. I have seen so many people treating a subordinate or secretary with disrespect. It is terrible to treat someone with less seniority as less of a person.

Remember this, even if you forget everything else in this book. The way you treat people is a strong reflection on you.

BELIEVE IN YOURSELF

Think what you can become.

So many people hold themselves back because down deep they don't believe they have the ability and capability to do the job or task at hand—or at least not as well as someone else does it. I think we always give other people the benefit of the doubt based on their background or history, yet we sell ourselves short. We don't know that they are actually nervous about doing something or that they really haven't done it before, but we know that we haven't. I believe this issue crops up all the time. So many times, I look at myself as just a regular person and can't believe how successful I have been. As positive a person as I am, I have been filled with self-doubt. I have had some great talks with Chris, in which she made me re-examine the facts and what I have achieved and really made me realized just how much I have accomplished, even if I don't think I am anyone special.

I have been shocked so many times when people have admitted to me how scared or nervous they were in a meeting or situation. They have actually stated that they had wished that I were doing the job. What a surprise! I assumed they were so confident that I was thinking how nice it was not to have to do it because I wasn't going to be as good or comfortable.

Remember, you are there for a reason. You've earned your success, and you should feel confident because of that.

BE POLITE

It costs nothing to be polite.
—Winston Churchill

Enron was a tough, competitive environment. I was very successful there although it was a constant challenge in many respects. In the late 1990s, trading became more and more dominant in earnings, growth and culture. One of the values that quickly went by the wayside was the day-to-day activity of being polite. As people became more powerful and successful, this was the first to go. So often people were treated poorly, manners or basic respect was set aside, and people wore rudeness almost like a badge of honor. Upper level employees treated lower level employees appallingly. As you become more successful, don't fall into that trap. A man should still hold the door for a woman, should be on time, say thank you and say hello or good morning. Nobody should put people down, yell, degrade them or even raise his or her voice in a group setting. Being polite and treating people with respect almost carried an air of weakness at Enron. I did all right for being so weak. Don't rationalize your way into dismissing anyone.

COMPLIMENT PEOPLE IN A CROWD

So much of good management is common sense. Everyone likes to get positive feedback. When there is an opportunity to compliment someone on his or her work, do so. You cannot ever fake it or make it up, though. It should be genuine. There are plenty of opportunities to find problems or negative items and you should make sure to point out a negative when necessary, but if negative comments aren't balanced with positive remarks when appropriate, people won't trust you and it will be impossible to attain loyalty. When I had floor meetings I always tried to make a point of laying out the good and the not so good. In the good, I tried to point out something especially positive that had happened or an achievement that exceeded expectations, including the responsible person or team. Dozens of times people have thanked me for mentioning their efforts or for pointing out something they had accomplished. It has a huge impact.

REMEMBER PEOPLE'S NAMES

This falls into the category of do as I say, not as I do. I am not good at this. In fact, it is a weakness of mine. People like to hear their names in conversation. Calling people by their names in a conversation makes it more personal; they can identify with it. In addition, whenever possible, mention names in a group setting. Again, people like the recognition and acknowledgement. One of the most popular executives at Enron was a man named Ron Burns. He was very talented at this skill and if he met you once, he remembered. People loved him and felt very loyal to him, because he cared enough to remember their names and something about them.

I encourage you to work very hard to achieve this skill. It will pay off in big ways, both personally and professionally.

INTRODUCE YOURSELF FIRST

Whether it is on the phone or in person, always be the first one to state your name. People respect that and it will open doors for you. With each call, I always start, no matter what level the individual is that I am calling, "This is Mike McConnell; is Rich available?" An assistant on the phone notices things like this and it conveys that you are not afraid to say who you are or that you are not a salesperson. I think this is a big deal. It is also about respect. You respect them and you are showing it.

People also really appreciate it. It may save them from embarrassment and gives them the chance to say something like, "Of course, we've met before," or, "Of course I remember." I think it could also become infectious and they may start doing it too, that would be a great trend.

SAY "NICE TO SEE YOU," NOT "NICE TO MEET YOU"

The more senior you get in the organization, the more people will probably work for you. I've directly managed 1,500 people at one time, too many for me to know everyone, especially because of my weakness for remembering names. I also made many speeches and got a lot of coverage in internal publications. People soon called me by name and I either didn't recognize them or was not sure who they were. Enron had 20,000 employees and I was one of the top officers, and my picture and stories were around a great deal. One very handy trick I learned was to greet people with, "Nice to see you," versus, "Nice to meet you." Quite often people used to tell me that we had met before and where it was. All I did by using the "meet" greeting was hurt their feelings or tell them that they weren't important enough to commit to memory. I saw this in action at a Christmas party while I was at HPL. One of my accountants came up to introduce me to his wife. He started out by saying hello and giving me his name and I said, "Merry Christmas; nice to meet you." He was devastated and embarrassed in front of his wife. I'm sure he told her that we knew each other well. I quickly recovered but once again learned my own lesson. I am sure that I had probably met him at some point, but regardless of that, I was never to make this mistake again. This rule has helped me many, many times.

SEND FLOWERS TO SPOUSES

I have always rewarded the spouses of my team members with a thank-you gift when people who worked on a big deal spent a lot of time on a project. They make sacrifices, too, and are often forgotten and don't share the reward or rush that comes from getting the deal closed. My assistant, Cathy Phillips—the best in the business—was great at remembering and following up on this type of special thank you. It made the spouses feel like part of the team, and they *were* a very important part of the team. Support at home is vital.

WRITE HAND-WRITTEN NOTES

Receiving a note of thanks, congratulations or recognition has made many people very happy. People really enjoy something personal. Taking even a few minutes and physically writing something is so different from a form letter or something that a secretary probably did. Even adding a small written note or sentence to a business letter has the same impact. When I was on the board of JDF and asked for money for our big fundraiser, I always made the letters very personal in nature, adding an individual comment by my signature. I had amazing success, well beyond my wildest dreams. Everyone sent me a donation. I raised close to $100,000. People really appreciated the personal nature and compassion.

Another key to my success was that I sent every single person, without fail, a hand-written thank-you note for supporting me. Many people commented on that for years. It was a real pain and commitment but it was worth it. I also discovered one day that my accountant had kept two notes that I wrote him when he did a good job helping close a big deal, and he displayed them with the deal toys that we handed out after we closed the transaction. Years later, they both are out there for everyone to read. That's an impact. It takes time to write notes but it is worth it. By the way, I still have every significant one that I ever received.

Chapter Three:

Organization

GOALS AND OBJECTIVES FOR WORK

If you don't know where you are going, any road will get you there.
—Lewis Carroll

I've discussed the importance of this earlier but setting out vision, strategy, mission statements and goals and objectives has been one of the key factors to my success at work. Develop these together with all the leaders in a business unit. If you develop them by yourself, you will fail. It will be your plan, not theirs. You can obviously have great influence on the process and of course the direction in which the group goes (that is your job as a leader), but it will be their goals and mission, not yours. You are one part of the process, just like the rest of the team. Your job in developing these specific goals is to facilitate and help make them complete and heading in the right direction, not to write them yourself.

After goals are fully developed, agreed upon and the commitment is made to accomplish them, then the employees are accountable for them. I always hold people accountable for their goals. I focused more on whether they reached their overall goals or objectives, rather than the specifics along the way. They had flexibility within the goals to manage their business. I was able to manage, review and keep up with overall progress on their success through this mechanism. I didn't have to micro-manage. There is no need to ask every day how they are doing. I would know how they were doing via tracking progress based on their goals and objectives. We also had quarterly reviews to amend or update our goals. Things change and change often, and you should update your goals, whether financial or strategic. This way of keeping up also made it easier to see obstacles before they became insurmountable. I was able to step in and help, sometimes before people knew they were struggling. This is a very powerful tool. It also isn't unique in business. It is commonplace as a general management tool, but most managers don't keep up or pay attention as they should along the way, even when things aren't going well. Also in most cases, the goals or vision are crammed down to the business people by upper management that "knows better." A huge mistake. This is more then simply setting up budgets.

Another important management tool I used was radar screens for each of my businesses. A radar screen was a one- or two-page set of information that provided an excellent summary of each area of focus or important piece of the business. Each group owns a portion of this radar screen. I also made it very reader friendly with a combination of graphs and numbers. Reports can be so dry and boring and thus much easier to ignore. It was vital to know and check monthly to see if problems were developing, and the screens were an excellent tool to fix the problem area. It also became a tool of friendly competition. Some competition is very good as long as it doesn't get out of hand. As a manager, I also liked watching how people reacted to this kind of pressure. It told me a great deal about them, how they handled problems and how they motivated, or blamed, others in their group.

I also discovered a great side benefit of the radar screens. I was able to send them to my bosses or key managers in the company to illustrate where my businesses were in relation to our plan. People could see firsthand where we stood and they developed confidence in our group. Second-guessing decreased and communication via these tools increased significantly. It also turned out to be very helpful to me personally because in the end, we usually made our plan and it made everyone in the group look good.

Set goals and objectives for work. You will improve over time and discover a great deal about your businesses and yourself at the same time.

BE ON TIME

This is a real pet peeve of mine. My schedule got more and more crowded every year. At times, I did need two assistants to keep up with everything I was doing. One thing I tried to maintain, however, was showing up to meetings on time. This was a terrible issue at Enron and meetings would start 30 minutes late while people were waiting around. It became common to bring plenty of other work with you so you could take care of other business while waiting. This gets back to respect as well. I don't think that most people did it as a power trip; most of it was bad planning or daily emergencies. I did know some people whom I believe did make you wait, just to illustrate their power. This is an old negotiation trick, and one I don't think people should use. Although I was late often to meetings, it wasn't from lack of trying, not that that is a proper excuse. I think you will find that you will have more effective meetings and will get on people's calendars a lot easier when you show up on time and show people the respect they deserve.

HAVE A GREAT ASSISTANT

As an executive, time management is extremely important and difficult. Having a great assistant to help you is very important. Upon my return from my London assignment, I inherited an assistant, although we both checked each other out thoroughly. Cathy Phillips set the standard for executive assistants. She was a great organizer and was a true member of my team. I don't know how I would have done my job without her. I respected her abilities and let her do her job. She had great ideas, so I listened to her and tried things. In almost every case (actually, I can't remember a single time that this didn't happen), we implemented or tried her new idea to save time or manage my day. One of the most effective procedures we put in place was our morning meeting. At 7:30 a.m. each day, we had a meeting to go over the day and prioritize items. She would bring in my calendar, print important e-mails, tell me people who wanted to see me and we would get the day started on the right track.

She was also the consummate professional. She dressed conservatively, was always "on" and one of her best attributes was something she didn't do. She never took advantage of the power she had, never. I cannot express to you how rare that is. It was hard enough for me to handle the power and prestige of the position. And, like anyone else, executive assistants have a strong tendency to enjoy their power and it affects their behavior. They become more and more difficult to work with outside the executive office. There is a delicate balance between protecting you and wielding this power over lower-ranked employees.

Watch out for assistants in general. Everyone has a tendency to believe that theirs is the best and when we would rank or discuss assistants in their performance reviews, it became very personal, very quickly. Oddly enough, most people don't even know when they have a bad assistant.

CARRY A POCKET INDEX CARD

The busier I got, the more difficult it was to keep up with my commitments. I found that I would meet someone in the hall and then later forget to call or send an e-mail or set up a meeting as I had promised to do. I then started a practice that has helped me for years. I began carrying an index card in my pocket, so I could stop and write down a chance commitment or needed piece of information. I also added a piece of my own personality by adding an affirmation at the top of the card. I would glance at that every time I got it out. My affirmation would also be reflective of what was important to me at the time. This really helped me to maintain a reputation that means a lot to me. I have always been known as someone who would live up to my commitments.

This practice also had an added benefit. I found that ideas would flow and I could immediately write them down. It also became a self-fulfilling prophecy. Since I had it around, my mind would constantly be thinking about ideas, which I knew I wouldn't forget.

Chapter Four:

Work

You will spend a large percentage of your life working—that is, if you want to be successful. We form our work habits very early in life. Think about your classmates, as far back as grade school, and you will be able to identify the ones destined for success. It is vital that you focus on your work; really focus. No faking it or going through the motions, or you will pay the price. Later in life, your family will also pay the price. Although much of the principles in this book can be applied directly to work habits, here are a few points that bear special attention.

PASSION

Passion persuades. Every time. If you really believe in something, people will want to be part of it. So many people just do what they are told or may try something different but don't do it with passion and people interpret that they aren't really committed to it. A great deal of my success comes from truly believing in what I was doing; people joined right in. They want to believe in something especially if your idea or concept makes sense.

DO WHAT IS ASKED AND OVER-DELIVER

Expectations are always very curious things. They really set the standards and—well—expectations. I haven't always been very good at following my own advice here. I had a tendency to jump out, put a big stake in the ground and make big promises. Fortunately, I delivered pretty well, although I sure did live dangerously. I also think that was important to me for setting lofty goals.

I have seen this very common mistake repeatedly, especially with very smart and young employees. When you have a task or assignment, make sure you do that assignment. Do specifically what was requested, not what you think should have been requested. This is a very subtle but important difference. You may not know exactly what your boss was thinking or where he was going with the request. I remember one very specific example that stuck with me over these many years. I had a very sharp associate in London who temporarily went to help the vice president responsible for all gas marketing in Europe. It was awful. She consistently refused to give the boss what he had asked for and instead produced a ton of work all around the issue. She was convinced that he didn't know what he was doing and she had a better idea of the project's needs. Well, she didn't and almost lost her job over it. That person never forgot how she acted. I didn't either. In fact, I was more tolerant than the other person was and didn't realize just how much I hadn't been getting what I had been asking for either. I did have several talks with her and she listened, changed her ways and became very successful at Enron and beyond.

The key to being a good, or rather great, employee is providing not only what your boss but also including your thoughts or other important data in your response. That kind of initiative, when properly channeled, will pay off ten-fold. Having additional factors to consider or a perspective really thought out or laid out is hugely valuable. That will make you successful at work.

OUTWORK THE COMPETITION

When it gets down to a key to my success in any position or project, one factor is very consistent. I simply worked very hard and outworked and out-prepared the competition. I was always ready and practiced what I needed to do. If it was important, I avoided "winging it." It gets down to work ethic and practice. Professional golfers don't leave their shot making to chance; they practice until their hands bleed. If I had to go through a big negotiation session, I would rehearse it, plan counter moves and choices, make lists of potential give-ins, look back at past trends and study what they have done in the past; be ready. You can't ever have all the answers but if the other party has to react totally and you have a plan, as well as an alternative plan and a list of ideas going in, you will be ready. Many times your plan isn't that useable or the course doesn't go your way but it will pay dividends even if it happens later or creates a subtle difference when you least expect it. At the very least, you are increasing the odds of success. That will pay off at some point.

NEVER UNDERESTIMATE YOUR OPPONENT

If you underestimate your opponent, this is a sure-fire formula for failure. Not every time, but often enough so that it matters. You may be better, but if you let your guard down or get cocky, there will be a payment. It may not—and probably won't—be when you expect it. There are millions of examples of this in life. One of my favorites is the Oklahoma Sooners. In 2000 the Sooners went 11–0 which was a complete surprise. It was not because of one superstar but because of teamwork, dedication and belief. My brother Mark and I went to the National Championship game at the Orange Bowl against Florida State. Even after beating five top ten teams, people gave us no chance to beat the once-defeated and defending champion Seminoles. People gave us absolutely no chance to win. In fact even after an amazing season, there was even talk that we shouldn't have even been invited to the game. FSU had obviously read the press and were convinced they would win and cover the 14-point spread. When they arrived on the field, you could see the difference. The Sooners were so fired up, I was concerned. FSU was very serious and matter-of-fact. The Sooners believed they could win. I've already gone over the power of belief but also the Sooners were completely ready, outworked the competition, didn't underestimate the opponent; quite the opposite they worked extra hard knowing the obstacle that was coming. They couldn't be stopped; even by FSU's Heisman Trophy-winning quarterback. OU beat them in every way. It was total domination and only a bad snap on a punt at the end of the game allowed FSU to score 2 points. It was a shut out and that hadn't happened to them in many years. It was one of the greatest events of my life. To this day, I am very thankful I went. I had many, many excuses why I didn't have time to go, but it was a great experience.

FOCUS ON GROWTH NOT EXPENSES

You cannot save your way into prosperity.

What actually drives success and business? Growth. You certainly don't cut your way to success. Watching the expenses in a business is important, but primary focus on that can kill a business, at least one that must show growth or one that must be cultivated. I always focus on gross margin versus earnings before interest and taxes (EBIT). EBIT is vital for more mature businesses, but if you are trying to change a culture or introduce a paradigm shift, you must move forward and close deals. Someone other than the CEO can cut or watch costs. This is not the CEO's function, and a CEO who focuses too much on this part of the business will eventually fail to achieve his real goals and objectives.

After the collapse of Enron, I took a retrospective study of the incredible waste in the Wholesale division. We were so wasteful and abusive of what we could spend. Everything was new and everyone—and I mean **everyone**—had to have the best new device or the latest version. Sometimes that was warranted, but usually it was not. I was caught up in it as well. I had the latest and greatest and tried many hand held devices and smaller and smaller laptop computers. It was part of the culture. We had a culture of arrogance and an in-your-face appearance of greatness. The most positive thing I can say is that I was by far the least abusive of my peers, but that doesn't give me much solace.

Expenses also hit the bottom line of your business. Those savings translate into cash flow. One of my lessons learned about running my businesses was too much focus on earnings before interest, taxes, depreciation and amortization (EBITDA). That was my key metric. My performance was measured against it, and I was supposed to manage the growth around it. I was to grow EBITDA and gross margin. I realize now that I completely underestimated the measurement of cash flow versus earnings. Even though I wasn't supposed to focus much on cash flow, I still should have. Make sure someone is watching the expenses and cash, if you are not doing it.

Cash flow is the key at the end of the day. The last time I checked you pay for your groceries with cash not earnings!

DRESS THE PART

Clothes don't make a person, but they do make up 90 percent of what you see of them. Look your best at all times.

I really enjoy the business world. From as far back as I remember, the days of going into the office with my dad, I thought everyone always looked very impressive, formal and fancy. That impression stuck with me when I joined the business world. From the very beginning of my work life, I always tried to look the best and the most professional that I could. So many people don't dress well and I think that this limits their career opportunities. I always thought that money spent on my business wardrobe was money well spent. In fact, I didn't normally worry too much about how much a tie cost or, within reason, a good suit. I also always wanted to look sharp and polished but also conservative. If fashion is not one of your strengths, ask for help. I don't just mean a salesperson, although they can certainly make sure you don't make a mistake, I mean ask someone at work. If a person always appears sharp or has that "air" about them and the way they dress, ask them where they shop or how they buy clothes. They won't mind and they will be flattered that you noticed. If that bothers you or makes you feel uncomfortable, go shopping and look at the mannequins or in the shop windows. In addition, catalogs can be very helpful. Buy exactly what you see, if you don't know what is best. There are several ways, but do something.

I think this is a very important business tip. I always looked good and at the very least, there were no negative issues with the way I looked. I took that one issue of potential company politics out of my world. It was also a sense of pride for me. I was doing something important and I ought to dress that way. It also gave me confidence and gave people confidence about me. No matter what social event, anyone I was around knew that I wouldn't embarrass him or her or give him or her any concern.

I always paid attention to this. Always. It came in very handy even on airplanes. I never wanted to look bad or scruffy. You never know whom you might sit next to on the plan. I have sat with many executives and friends of friends. It is absolutely worth the effort.

Genius is 1% inspiration, 99% perspiration.
—Thomas Edison

The big shots are only the little shots that keep shooting.
—Christopher Morley

You must pay the price if you wish to secure the blessings.
—Andrew Jackson

A diamond is a piece of coal that stuck to the job.
—Malcolm Forbes

There is plenty of room at the top, but there's no room to sit down.
—Toastmasters

Nothing motivates a man more than to see his boss putting in an honest days work.
—Unknown

Work hard and become a leader; be lazy and never succeed.
—Proverbs 12:24

Work is the salt that gives life flavor.
—Unknown

Grant me the courage not to give up even thought I think it is hopeless.
—Chester W. Nimitz

A good beginning is half the battle.
—Unknown

You reap what you sow.
—Galatians 6:7

Opportunity is missed by most people because it is dressed in overalls and looks like work.
—Thomas Edison

When the going gets tough, the tough get going.
—Joseph Kennedy

Hard work brings prosperity; playing around brings poverty.
—Proverbs 28:19

There is honor in doing your best.
—Unknown

WORK ETHIC

No one ever drowned in sweat.
—Lou Holtz

My father once told me, "If you are tired at the end of a work day, then you earned your salary." I can honestly say that I must have earned a lot. My approach to work is that I really feel I owe the company my best every minute. I do get tired and unmotivated at certain times but that expression always comes back to me. My wife certainly believes that it gets in the way and dominates my life. I really do feel, with my very high compensation, that the company has a right to expect me to be "on" all the time. When I earned a normal type of salary and overall compensation, I didn't feel it as strongly but now I do feel as if they rather own me, and my total commitment. I don't know that I'm right here but from a work perspective, it has treated me pretty well.

So many times, I was against some very intelligent and worthy adversaries in a negotiation. Rarely, however, was I ever out-maneuvered, because I out-worked or out-prepared them every time. "Practice makes perfect" is an old adage and it is certainly true in the business world as well. I "practiced" or continued studying, rehearsing, or thinking of alternatives. All the work paid off repeatedly. Hard work does pay off and don't ever doubt that. The discipline of your work ethic becomes part of you and allows you to reach deep down when you need it. That doesn't mean that you are physically aware of it, but you somehow get the winning idea or find that the right answer pops into your mind for the situation.

Another benefit for those who work hard and have a strong work ethic is that people want to be around people who work hard. Other strong and successful people respect them and are drawn to them. In addition, people really want someone like that as part of a team. Also, you get the benefit of getting more chances or breaks. If you do make a mistake or things don't go your way in a big project or transaction, people have a tendency to give you another chance or overlook the error. You've earned that break. Many people in this world are so talented and brilliant that they can fake working hard and still be very successful. However, when those people have issues or problems, others will not stick up for them because down deep people have no respect for their work ethic. You may respect them in other ways, but you wonder if they would have failed at the task if they really put out a lot of effort or worked harder.

There is also another benefit. When opportunities come up, especially opportunities that you don't even know about, you will be considered for that promotion, new job or transfer because of your work ethic and the kind of person you are down deep. Working hard is a great management motivation tool because you really do lead by example. If you work hard, it is a guarantee that your staff will work harder in response. The same of course goes with the other side of the coin. By the way, when those opportunities do pop up unexpectedly or another company offers you a big promotion or the job of your dreams, enjoy it. You've earned it.

Turn stumbling blocks into stepping-stones.
—Unknown

The difference between ordinary and extraordinary is the little "extra."
—Jimmy Johnson

The hero is not braver than an ordinary man, but he is brave five minutes longer.
—Ralph Waldo Emerson

You will never stub your toe standing still but the faster you go, the more chance you have of getting somewhere.
—Charles Kettering

A champion is someone who gets up even when they can't.
—Jack Dempsey

It's hard to beat a person who never gives up.
—Babe Ruth

Victories often occur after you see no way to succeed but refuse to give up anyway.
—Dave Weinbaum

Patience is the toughest road to stay on, but the surest path to victory.
—Dave Weinbaum

Ninety percent of those who fail are not actually defeated. They simply quit.
—Paul J. Meyer

Nothing is easy to the unwilling.
—Nikki Giovanni

The only place where success comes before work is in the dictionary.
—Donald Kendall

Success is not getting to the top—but how you bounce on the bottom that counts.
—George S. Patton

Some people dream of success, while others wake up and work hard at it.
—Mary Martin

Life has two rules: Number one, never quit; Number two, always remember rule number one.
—Duke Ellington

DON'T GIVE UP

I have had the good fortune to work on many very big issues and problems. I say good fortune because it taught me firsthand not to give up and to persevere. When you believe in something and you are running into serious roadblocks or obstacles, keep going. They are signals of what is not working, not to stop and quit. Even if at the end of the day, you decide to take something in a new direction or that things have changed and it is time to stop, decide that it is time to make that change; don't quit. Don't ever be a quitter.

Work as if you can't fail. In two of my jobs, the FP&L and J-Block negotiations, failure was not an option. When you know you're right, you must be the Rocky Balboa of the job. Not having the option of quitting makes you stronger and drives you harder to find a way to make it work. It is great to be known as someone who is very diligent. Everyone appreciates someone who keeps going when the going is tough. People want to be around committed people. Life and jobs are not a sprint. Be a marathon runner.

There are times when you clearly must cut your losses. Sometimes people stop things for you. Make sure that you don't give up simply for the sake of giving up. Being tired or frustrated is not the answer or an excuse to walk away. Think about all the things that would have or would not have happened in this world if people had given up. Every performance review I've ever seen lists diligence as an important attribute. Live up to that.

So many people simply quit because the job gets hard or frustrating. Be the person that doesn't quit, the one who keeps going and wins.

I can't emphasize this enough. There are so many great examples of this in the history of the world. Thousands of stories tell us about people who quit just before achieving success. You can't be one of these people. Read books about this. The stories are real and are better than fiction. A writer couldn't create a story as good as what real people have done in desperate situations. Read these affirmations carefully and often. Living up to them is truly a life-changing event. One of my favorite stories is about Winston Churchill. Reading his speeches, touring his war room in London, listening to his radio addresses, learning his daily regime is all very inspiring. They are not only inspiring but we owe our lives to him. I truly believe that if he hadn't done everything he did, and I mean everything, we would most likely be speaking German and most of us in my generation wouldn't exist. I shudder to think about the outcome of World War II without the British hanging in there and surviving while America came around. That is leadership. That is taking the hard road because it was the right thing to do. We all have to live up to our own tiny version of his decisions. Are you up to the task? Are you going to hang in there and do what is right? Be that person. If Churchill had taken shortcuts or any of the possible easy ways out, America wouldn't be the way it is today.

There are times in our lives when we have to survive one day at a time. There is nothing wrong with it; it is merely life. If you think about life being 80 years long, don't you really expect that there will be times, even long stretches, of very difficult or terrible times? Perseverance and diligence are the only ways to keep going and move on through those times and come out the other side.

He that will not sail until all dangers are over must never put to sea.
—T. Fuller

You can't steal second base and keep one foot on first.
—Unknown

In America, anyone can become president. That's one of the risks you take.
—Adlai Stevenson

If everyone is thinking alike then somebody isn't thinking.
—George S. Patton

Imagination is more important than knowledge.
—Albert Einstein

Opportunities are seldom labeled.
—John A. Shedd

And the trouble is, if you don't risk anything you risk even more.
—Erica Jong

The person who will risk nothing ... does nothing, has nothing, is nothing. Only a person who risks becomes truly free.
—Leo Buscaglia

In the middle of difficulty lies opportunity.
—Albert Einstein

Nothing in life is to be feared. It is only to be understood.
—Marie Curie

Life is like riding a bicycle. You don't fall off unless you stop pedaling.
—Claude Pepper

If you life is free from failures, you're not taking enough risks.
—H. Jackson Brown, Jr.

Unless you try to do something beyond what you have already mastered, you will never grow.
—Ralph Waldo Emerson

Grab a chance and you won't be sorry for a might have been.
—Arthur Ransome

PLAN YOUR OWN CAREER AND TAKE RISKS

Your future is yours alone. Most modern companies leave a person's career path up to the individual. Over the years, the old management style and philosophy of selecting a path and moving people around in a regimented fashion has vanished. With the exception of analyst and associate programs, which many times still offer the candidate a great deal of control on a rotation, it's up to you. You must design your own path. Think about trying something different; don't always follow the money but follow what you want to do and how you know you can add value. Tell your boss your interests. Go for jobs in other departments or begin the process by meeting people in an area in which you are interested. Take jobs that give you a shot. Take risks. Obviously, you must be sensitive to your individual boss' personality, but most will not take offense. In fact, I would challenge you to move or gravitate away from a supervisor that would block a promotion or new opportunity within the company.

As a manger, I almost always encourage people to follow their interests or desires to make a change. If I don't, they may get stale and leave the company anyway, out of boredom or frustration. It is better to keep them working at the company and get value for the shareholders. I have also made it a point to step in sometimes and let people know the risks. Some were walking into disaster and couldn't see it. I've never stopped opportunities for someone, but if I was convinced it wouldn't work due to skill sets or extreme personality conflicts, I would talk to them about it. Remember: It is their life not yours. If it doesn't work out, it was their choice and you gave them honest advice. I couldn't possibly relay all my examples of letting people move on to other things even when it hurt our group for a while, but I don't regret a single time. Many of those people know or found out how I quietly helped them and have come back to me with very sincere thanks. I do love helping people. I really do believe in helping all and enjoy seeing their growth and benefits even if they are only internal. I've also learned of promotions and big raises that my boss at the time has stopped without my knowledge. I still resent it today and don't ever want someone thinking this way about me.

Taking risks in your career and doing something that people don't want to take on or fear is a real key to succeeding and moving up the corporate ladder. Solving an impossible problem, fixing an organization, matching your skills with something that really needs doing and being willing to be very visible is a great combination. It is also a scary combination. You can easily fail as well. You must have the confidence and, more importantly, the support of your superiors; real support. I took on many very "risky" career moves but in each case, I knew that I had real support and the availability of good resources. Resources equal support in the business world.

My opportunity to go to England and work on the J-Block problem was a case in point. I was very nervous about moving out of the country and risking my successful career, which was really on a roll. I had just solved the Florida Power and Light issue, which was Enron's number one corporate goal in 1992, then generated $60 million in earnings by buying the Pan National and Amoco contracts from Citrus Trading into Enron Gas Marketing. I couldn't have had a better year. I was destined to become a vice president at year-end and receive a big bonus. Then the London opportunity came along. To make it even worse, I had to discuss it with Chris on the very day she came home from the hospital from delivering Michael, our second child. That was a difficult conversation. I talked about the job with many of my friends and got opinions from some of Enron's top executives. Not one single person thought I should take the job! Not one. I knew in my gut I could do it and that it was an opportunity I shouldn't pass by. I knew I could add value to the company. It turned out to be one of the most significant decisions I ever made and that is an understatement.

I had a similar experience upon my repatriation back to the US after we successfully completed the J-Block transaction in July 1997. I had many different job opportunities presented to me, although that is not to say it was an easy process. It was a great problem to have. One opportunity presented itself that I again knew I could do and that would give me the highest visibility in the company. I took the job as president of Houston Pipeline and Louisiana Resources Company. Again, just like in 1993, not a single person thought I should take the job; everyone thought it was too far-gone and old school. Not only was it a great job and one that worked out to be very successful, but it was also the most fun I ever had.

Each one of these opportunities involved taking real perceived risk. I went for it and it paid off beyond my wildest dreams.

If you're not moving forward, you're moving backward.
—Unknown

Things may come to those who wait but only those things left by those who hustle.
—Abraham Lincoln

Action cures fear.
—Dr. David J. Schwartz

Take action, only action provides results.
—Unknown

Don't wait for your ship to come in, swim out to it.
—Unknown

Vehicles in motion use their generators to charge their own batteries.
—Malcolm Forbes

Sow an action, reap a habit. Sow a habit, reap character. Sow character, reap a destiny.
—William Makepeace Thackeray

Just do it.
—Nike

A journey of 1,000 miles begins with a single step.
—Chinese Proverb

Parking meters should remind us that we lose money standing still.
—Unknown

Desire is a treasure map. Knowledge is the treasure chest. Wisdom is the jewel. Yet, without action, they all stay buried.
—Pliny the Elder

Get good counsel before you begin; and when you have decided, act promptly.
—Sallust

The way to get started is to quit talking and begin doing.
—Walt Disney

2/3 of promotion is motion.
—Unknown

ACTIONS SPEAK LOUDER THAN WORDS

It is very important to be biased toward action versus study or analysis. Many very smart people over-analyze a situation or event and it can paralyze them. Action and moving forward are vital. Action changes the events as they come and forces re-examination and new decision-making. You can always change your mind and once again take action in a new direction if you are wrong or something simply isn't working.

People also watch much more closely than they listen. You may say one thing and do another. The "other" will influence the most people every time. The expression, "Walk the talk" really is important. In fact, if you don't "walk the talk," you will lose credibility and actually take the team backwards. No one wants to be around a "talker" versus a "do-er." The world is full of people who don't want to work but want to show how smart they are. This doesn't get the job done. Some would say that there is a profession for people like this: College professor. Whether it is your children or your employees, no one likes a hypocrite. The message that will ultimately be transmitted is what you do, not what you say.

If you are not willing to pay the price with action, then you are not really committed to what ever it is. It is easy to talk a good game but quite another to play a good game. In addition, action equals accountability. If you are actively working it, you must be committed and willing to take accountability for your actions. When you combine action with passion, it is a powerful force and one that others will notice.

Action = Investment. Once you lose this kind of credibility, it will be very difficult to get it back. People will notice, good or bad. If you talk about working hard but you leave work at 5 p.m., you've lost credibility. This relates to leading by example.

Action also conquers fears. People miss that point. You have to confront your fears in order to conquer them. And, you can't confront something passively, can you?

Chapter Five:

Speed

MOVE FASTER THAN YOU THINK YOU SHOULD

Move forward, always. Play defense very cautiously. Unless you will have dire consequences or very difficult circumstances, try something, make a decision and take action. One example that comes to mind is when it comes to big organization changes almost everyone agrees that those changes should have gone faster than they did. When I was President of HPL, I knew that I needed to make a change on one person but I didn't have any proof that he was really the problem. Finally, I fired him over an event of clear insubordination and all the "proof" I needed came pouring out. I wished that I had moved faster and followed my gut call. I do regret not making the call and keeping other employees intimidated and quietly miserable. Not bad for an only regret. Of course, this doesn't mean you should treat people unfairly. Be fair, but be fast. Being an action-taker sends a signal to the organization, which is healthy as well. People respect someone who takes accountability and moves the business forward. Again, as long as people think you made the decisions thoughtfully and fairly, speed wins big. Your gut or intuition is usually right. Follow your gut and thoughts.

One key element to moving quickly and having people follow is to communicate and communicate often. People will be more likely to trust you and give you the benefit of the doubt if they know you have a plan and aren't acting for speed's sake. People also learn something about you if you don't take the action. Tolerating incompetence sends a strong signal. You have to get the right people on the bus and the wrong people off the bus, or those onboard will resent it.

WALK FAST

This may seem an odd topic, but I do think it has served me well. I believe that I first heard of this from a tape series from Anthony Robbins, *Unlimited Power*. One of his points was that by walking fast, you would be confident and purposeful. It is a reflection of you. Whether the walk caused the confidence or vice versa, I do think there is a cause-and-effect relationship.

Does a person sing because he is happy or is he happy because he is singing? Cause and effect is an odd pair. One thing you can't do is deny there is a relationship between events and actions. Walking fast became second nature to me at some point. In fact, people said they knew when I was coming and that I had a distinct "gait." Try this. I don't think there is any downside to trying it and seeing if it has a positive effect on you.

DON'T GO TO SOMEDAY-ISLE
—DENIS WAITLEY

Do It Now

I have remembered it ever since I first heard it from Dr. Waitley. It is very easy to put things of—even things that you really want to do. It is so easy to do. We all become so caught up in our lives and we put many things off. Big and little things. You don't want to go through life and be full of regrets. Anthony Robbins had another lesson that I have thought about often. It's called the rocking chair test. Try to think 40 years ahead when you make a big decision. Is this something that you would think about or be glad that you did while sitting in your rocking chair at 80? If it is, do it. If it isn't and you aren't sure what to do, or you must choose between a couple of options, let that be part of the decision. I think it works. If you apply this test, you won't go to Someday-Isle.

Chapter Six:

Decisions

GO BIG OR GO HOME

If it is worth doing, it is worth doing in a big way. At least prepare to do it in a big way. Very often, people jump in too big, but you should be ready to quickly expand and set up benchmarks and if they start proving out, go all the way. People can get excited and passionate about doing something big or significant. In addition, if it seems a small or insignificant effort, you won't be able to attract the best people.

One of my favorite comments about this philosophy is that you won't be dabbling at whatever you are doing. Thinking big and acting big changes your entire approach. People have a tendency to meet expectations whether they are big or small. Why not set big expectations? I could write an entire book about the negative effects of setting the bar too low, thus actually encouraging mediocre results and behaviors. We have that flawed philosophy in our public school systems right now. The key here is working toward something big or bigger. It will affect every decision and action that you take. You don't have to gamble the company to think and act big, just know how big you can be and what the possibilities are. I was able to use this philosophy when I took over and formed Enron Global Markets. The new company had nine different global trading businesses in it, but they all had one thing in common. Each business unit—and all of them were in different stages of their life cycles—believed it was non-core and unimportant. One of my first steps was to change that perspective. Smart and aggressive business people ran all the groups but they still all thought they were stepchildren in the family of Enron. I immediately changed their thinking and proved just how important these businesses were to the future of the entire company. They then began acting core and as if they were as important as the natural gas and power groups. All the businesses grew enormously and had an incredible future—one that included hyper-growth and expansion. With the incredible collapse of the company, these businesses fell the hardest. As I was making a speech to all my employees on what turned out to be the last gathering of the Enron Global Markets group, I thought of this philosophy, or mantra. My chief operating officer said, "Well Mike, you said, go big or go home; I guess we are going home." He meant it in fun, but everyone knew that we had given it our all. We had created something special and we were big.

Another aspect of the big is "big focus" not just scale. Be great at what you do. If you dabble, you can be mediocre. Asking yourself what you can be great at will clarify whether you should go big or go home.

GOING FOR IT

Shoot for the moon. Even if you miss it, you will land among the stars.
—Various

If you are going to do something, do it right and do it large. If you are going to do something, make an impact. Don't dabble. Do it right and make it big. Intense focus and a big plan produce big results. People put invisible leashes on themselves, and they don't know just how successful they can be. When I took over and created EGM, all the businesses had believed they were small and insignificant or unimportant. My first priority was to change that and push people to think outside the box and think and dream just how big or important they could be. It worked. The team was very talented, but the organization was actually holding them back largely. Setting high expectations and expecting them to perform and not to just grow a little each year but become a major business made a big difference. Whatever you do in life, do it big and with passion.

Earnings increased across the board even though we had the standard issue of a growing company. Every single business grew in deal flow and earnings. People really want to be part of success; sometimes they really just need the encouragement. In one of my last meetings before the Enron bankruptcy, we went through an interesting exercise. I flew all my managing directors and business unit heads to an executive offsite in Cabo San Lucas. It was a fancy trip but a great venue to develop big plans. I asked everyone, "How do we get our gross margin up to $1 billion?" A billion dollars! They were floored and thought I was crazy, but I explained that I recognized we couldn't do it the way we were operating today. What dramatic shifts or actions had to occur for us to reach that milestone? Some people immediately stated we couldn't do it no matter what. I said, "Well what if we could?" Many then responded that Enron's leadership hated assets. My response was simple. If we could illustrate how we would get to a billion dollars gross margin, wouldn't a very smart person at least consider our "new" way of doing it? Oddly enough, that part of the meeting never finished. Early on in that discussion, someone brought in a fax that addressed Enron's collapsing stock price with the $1 billion equity reclassification. Little did we know that very day was the beginning of the end of one of the most successful companies in that last decade. People today still can't believe how suddenly this collapse came about and the common view was that all the senior people had to know what was going on. This was a great example of how that wasn't the case. Within 40 days of that discussion, a discussion on how to make $1 billion in 2003, we were bankrupt, and I had blown up each one of those businesses. I went home on day 44.

REMEMBER: NOT MAKING A DECISION IS A DECISION

Don't wait for your ship to come in, swim out to it.
—Unknown

This is an important fact. Many people really have a hard time making decisions. They really struggle with making the "big" call, even if it actually wasn't very big at all. But, they forget one small thing. Not making a decision is making a decision. Sometimes doing nothing is the right course, but make sure you are making the decision not to make the decision. I quite often let things take their natural course to see what happens or because I didn't have enough facts. Watching what happens next allows you to make the next decision and take it back or in a new direction again, if necessary. Avoiding decisions for the sake of avoiding is normally not the right call. Why let destiny direct your future? Instead, be proactive and attempt to manage the process. You direct the future. Remember, you can't affect the direction of the wind but you can adjust your sails.

DON'T LOOK BACK

It is always easier to say this than it is to do it. You will do so many things and make thousands of decisions. Everything looks different in the rear view mirror and with 20/20 hindsight. As I look back over the biggest business decisions almost all of them look very different after a couple of years. By the way, some look even better than was expected also!

In my London assignment, I completed the J-Block negotiations and we dramatically changed our obligations under the contract. Very few people really knew what had happened and what we had accomplished in that deal. In fact, it sent some interesting shock waves throughout a very opinionated company. We paid out $450 million in cash as partial consideration of those 3-year negotiations. That was a huge number and because of it, we missed our quarterly earnings targets. That hadn't happened in many years and people, employees, were very upset. The analysts weren't however; the stock actually went up a $1/share upon the announcement of the settlement via a press release. That should have told people something but many didn't pick it up. The other signal that most people didn't pick up was that the company actually promoted me immediately when I came back into the United States. I became the new president of our North America unregulated pipelines. I was in an elevator one day after my return and two people who obviously didn't know me were talking about the J-Block deal. They were discussing the stupid deal we did and how it had hurt us. They were simply ignorant of the situation yet were very willing to provide their strong commentary.

I now realize closing that deal was a huge accomplishment that led to the amazing growth of the European operations and put an enormous liability behind the company. It may have even averted the death of the company and allowed it to take off over the next couple of years. Think about those people in the elevator when you want to criticize someone. They should have been thanking me instead of potentially hurting more than my feelings. One of those two guys later interviewed with me to join my group. We ended up bringing him into the group, but it sure would have been easy to hold a grudge.

BURN THE SHIPS

This is an expression from the explorer Cortez, I believe, and one that I really like. When you make a decision that you really believe is the right path, don't let people be indecisive. Make them go after the task with 100 percent effort. Once a person is in and agrees with the path, make them commit all the way. Take the easy exits away. People will be more dedicated and accomplish great things.

Experience is the name we give to our mistakes.
—Oscar Wilde

Go with your intuition.
—Unknown

Experience is not what happens to you. It is what you do with what happens to you.
—Aldous Huxley

Confidence is the inner voice that says you are becoming what you are capable of being.
—Unknown

Difficulties mastered are opportunities won.
—Winston Churchill

All decisions are made on insufficient evidence.
—Unknown

You are only courageous when you do what you feel is right despite your fear. Everyone feels fear, so everyone can be courageous.
—Unknown

If you listen to what you know instinctively, it will always lead you down the right path.
—Henry Winkler

Experience isn't interesting until it begins to repeat itself—in fact, until it does that, it hardly is experience.
—Elizabeth Bowen

These people are like … a frog living in a well, which has never seen the outside world. He knows only his well, so he will not believe that there is such a thing as the world. Likewise, people talk so much about the world because they have not known the joy of God.
—Unknown

He, who tastes not, knows not.
—Sufi Parable

It doesn't work to leap a twenty-foot chasm in two ten-foot leaps.
—American Proverb

There is no security on this earth. Only opportunity.
—Douglas McArthur

GO WITH YOUR GUT

Your gut isn't merely a feeling. It is experience talking. Rarely have I been wrong when my gut call was strong, even when I didn't have many facts to back it. Of course, you should not do things that may hurt people, based on a gut call. However, I can't remember a single time I felt something was wrong with a person and it turned out to be wrong. I'm talking about big things and situations in which I had some facts. I'm talking about really knowing and being directly involved in a situation, experience (another name for your gut call) is usually right.

As you move in a direction or make a decision, don't ignore feedback or facts as they develop. Gut calls are often vital where the facts are missing or not applicable, and you shouldn't ignore them. Be careful with this, especially if you are young or relatively inexperienced in a new job or situation. It is easy to confuse feelings with your gut. If logic and experience is trying to tell you something, listen carefully.

Don't be afraid to make the call and go with the gut. Remember if you do what is right, you can't go too far in the wrong direction. You can always correct the problem if you made a decision that doesn't turn out the way you had expected. Mistakes are generally easy to correct if they are made with the right intent and for the right reasons. Doing what is right helps you make the right choices.

I had an experience that really stands out and taught me this lesson well. I had just taken over as president of Houston Pipe Line. I had a vice president with a great background, and the group was working with moderate success but something didn't seem quite right. As the months passed, my feelings got stronger, but this particular person managed upwards very well. When things didn't go right, he always had an excellent excuse. He often did things that I didn't really like but, again, he always had a good story.

Finally, we put in place some financial guidelines that stated we would not make any company commitments without the head of Finance knowing the true impact of a proposal. This vice president violated the policy—badly—right off the bat. In fact, it felt intentional. I had to make a decision. I decided it was time for him to go, and I gave him the choice to leave the company and pursue other opportunities. He left, stunned and quietly angry. Then the floodgates of stories opened. He actually had been a huge problem and was carefully intimidating many people, especially his younger employees. My group was watching this termination and knew that, although I was a good person and wasn't rash, I meant what I said and wouldn't put up with that kind of attitude.

Go with your gut; it will rarely lead you astray.

Chapter Seven:

Leadership and Teamwork

I could write an entire book on this subject alone. In fact, many people already have, and you can find dozens of these books at any bookstore or online. The concept itself is not that complicated; the difficulty often lies in identifying leadership qualities. This is something I believe companies get wrong nearly 80 percent of the time. The most common mistake is making a leader out of someone who is the best at what he or she does, not because of his or her leadership skills. For example, a CPA firm might promote their best audit person to head the Audit department, but this person may not have the qualities required to lead a team. True, he or she may know Audit inside and out, but unless he or she has the right combination of vision, motivation, and people skills, it will be a bad decision on the part of management.

True leaders have an almost intangible quality, a distinctive air about them. Some call it a "cult of personality"; others simply refer to it as charisma. You can test this by simply observing the leaders around you. They might be executives at your company, community leaders, teammates, or even friends and acquaintances. Ask yourself how they became leaders. Was it because of hard skills, such as finance or accounting? Was leadership given to them, or did they take it on their own? Do they inspire their teams to do well, or do they lead by fear and intimidation? I guarantee the answers will surprise you. The following advice will help you realize your leadership potential.

SURROUND YOURSELF WITH THE BEST PEOPLE

Surround yourself with the best people possible. There is an old expression; "A" players surround themselves with "A" players; "B" players surround themselves with "C" players. I have seen this so many times. This is not an easy concept when it comes to work. I have always taken the philosophy of having outstanding people around, people who could take my place. This philosophy scares most people, and it makes everyone a little paranoid occasionally, but it is the absolute right thing to do. First, you can learn from them and the entire team gets better. Those people have an effect on all their people or the people they are involved with and, before long, the entire organization is stepping up. In addition, it insures your own success. How could you fail with a large number of very smart, dedicated and effective people surrounding you? It almost seems unfair. Also, if your people are that good, you can move on to another job or be promoted without the organization falling apart. I have benefited from this often. This is the upside to having all of these people capable of replacing you.

When you have thoroughbred horses, let them run. Only a poor manger would constantly rein them in. I believe this is one of America's biggest management issues. So many people get this wrong.

This section could be one of the most important management areas in the entire book. You have to get the right people on the bus. Just as important, you must get the wrong people off the bus. While editing this book, I read a very good book, actually a great book that addresses this very topic. The book is *Good to Great* by Jim Collins and he really hit this concept hard. You have to have the right people drive the bus. We used that expression very often when ranking and discussing our commercial people at Enron. The right people should not only get on the bus but should drive it to success.

Another key fact here is to recognize them and pay them. In fact, "over" pay them. A mistake that I have seen constantly by dozens of business heads is to negotiate very hard over a little amount of salary. If a real potential player wants to be paid $150,000 a year but you only want to pay him up to $145,000, what in the world does it matter? Even a much larger number doesn't make a real difference if it isn't messing up your pay scales. I would still say to do it and begin the process of improving those pay scales. Markets change and so may your scale. I would much rather give in and pay him what he wants and tell him he is worth it and you want him on your team. He will remember you stepped up and you and the company will reap the rewards later. I actually had an occasion to go to a president's house to negotiate a job promotion and salary increase and he wouldn't give me an extra $2,000, which would bring me up to only the mid point of the salary range within his company! I have remembered that moment for 15 years and still look at him and shake my head. He also told me that he really needed me on that night but wasn't going to give me the money. Not good management. He and I are both very lucky I let that go and didn't let it affect my performance. But, I still remember, even today.

SHARE CREDIT EVERY TIME

The way to get things done is not to mind who gets the credit of doing them.
—Benjamin Jowett

Give credit where credit is due. When people know that rewards will come, not only in money but also in admiration and recommendations, they will work harder and smarter. This will also create a trust that will last for years. It has come back to me years after a person has left my group and stopped me to say nice things or that he has adopted the same style or view. Even during the complete meltdown at Enron, treating people with dignity and recognizing them for their hard work and abilities created a loyalty that lived through the most difficult times of even telling people that they were going to lose their jobs; loyalty after the fact. Loyalty when they have nothing to gain by being loyal.

People will also follow you during hard times when there isn't a lot of credit to give. It therefore means that you take the blame and are truly accountable for the group's responsibilities. I remember one mid-level executive at Enron who didn't give or share credit, and when the going got tough, people not only left him hanging out to dry, they pushed him out. Not only did he not share credit, he actually believed he was the reason for everyone's success.

Sharing credit is simply the right thing to do.

Leadership is not exercising your authority.
—Unknown

Leaders change the changeable, accept the unchangeable and
remove themselves from the unacceptable.
—Denis Waitley

The price of greatness is responsibility.
—Winston Churchill

A leader is a dealer in hope.
—Napoleon Bonaparte

Leadership is the ability to translate vision into reality.
—Warren G. Bennis

Leaders are like eagles, they don't flock; you find them one at a time.
—Unknown

It's the job of a leader to make it easy to do the right thing, difficult to
do the wrong thing.
—Unknown

Lead the troops by action, not by words.
—Unknown

Leadership cannot really be taught. It can only be learned.
—Harold S. Geneen

What I do best is share my enthusiasm.
—Bill Gates

No man will make a great leader who wants to do it all himself, or to
get all the credit for doing it.
—Andrew Carnegie

Know your qualifications; realize your responsibilities; grasp your
opportunities; banish fear to the sidelines and success is inevitable.
—Jerome A. Waterman

Outstanding leaders go out of the way to boost the self-esteem of their
personnel. If people believe in themselves, it's amazing what
they can accomplish.
—Sam Walton

LEAD BY EXAMPLE

If you don't do this, how can you expect anyone else to do it? You must give a damn and step up. I always feel that I must work the hardest or have the most commitment. If the boss is the first one in the office and works the longest hours it is natural that other people will follow his or her lead. It is also a reflection on commitment to the job or to the company. If the leader doesn't care, no one else will either. Leadership is more than putting in time, but its effect shouldn't be underestimated.

It's also about the attitude and actions of the leader: body language, confidence, the entire package. People want to be lead and be successful. Helping people believe in themselves and working for a cause is a very powerful thing. If it is properly structured, they can accomplish great things.

The key to leadership is bringing out the best in people. It is the ability to have a vision, then share your vision with others and execute the plans to turn it into a reality. With an entire workforce or staff working in one direction with passion, it is actually hard to fail. One interesting part of leadership is examining the people who are around a leader. Does he attract the best and right kind of people? It will tell you a lot about which areas of the company will be successful. If your top talent is attracted to an idea or business, a leader must pay attention, then feed that opportunity, and bring out the best in it. Bad leadership so often actually kills good ideas and stifles growth. Being observant, attracting strong people and allowing them to be successful is so much of the battle.

One key focus for me that really contributed to being successful in a very innovative and often ruthless company was that I didn't try to take the credit. My job was to help people succeed. Many times, I did numerous things to help them or their group without them even knowing. Ultimately, they were successful. The next time they didn't need my help! The ability to see obstacles and knock them down *before* others do is a key to being a good manger. The ability to anticipating issues and think things through from a higher perspective is a welcome balance for someone engrossed in the detail level of a deal.

Show them how good they are. They don't usually realize it.

TEAM: <u>T</u>ogether <u>E</u>veryone <u>A</u>chieves <u>M</u>ore
—Unknown

Working together works.
—Unknown

I use not only all the brains I have, but all I can borrow.
—Woodrow Wilson

When spider webs unite, they can tie up a lion.
—Ethiopian Proverb

Teamwork is the highest form of accountability.
—Unknown

Only from the alliance of everyone working with each other are great things born.
—Antoine de Saint-Exupery

Teamwork divides the effort and multiplies the result.
—Unknown

You have to think "we" more than you think "me."
—Unknown

There is literally nothing that energizes, unites, and satisfies the family like working together to make a significant contribution.
—Unknown

No man will make a great leader who wants to do it all himself, or to get all the credit for doing it.
—Andrew Carnegie

It is amazing what you can accomplish if you do not care who gets the credit.
—Harry S. Truman

Great discoveries and improvements invariably involve the cooperation of many minds.
—Alexander Graham Bell

The ultimate test of a relationship is to disagree but to hold hands.
—Alexandria Penney

People support what they help create.
—Unknown

TEAMWORK

Teamwork is the key to success and producing the best work product. You can't confuse teamwork with taking command and leadership, however. Even the smartest people in the world would be better with other minds working on a problem or job. Five focused people working on a task is better than one genius. Dynamics also change, and if the team is focused and diverse, powerful things can happen. I've seen this over and over again. This is especially true if you select the people on the team for their strengths and ability to work together with different skill sets. If you should get someone who has a negative effect on the team, you must then take action to change the dynamic. Just as a good mix or great individual will really bring the group up and raise the bar, a bad person can have the opposite destructive effect as well. Employees regard failure to take action as bad management and acceptance of bad work habits.

A great aspect of teamwork is the network effect of having many people working on a project. The positive effects are definitely not linear. All of these individuals working toward a goal will have the effect of positive teamwork; the gains are exponential. Achievements come easier and in breakthroughs rather than through incremental progress.

Another bonus of teamwork is the power of each player pushing one another. That is why the group dynamics are so important. Accountability and non-destructive competition can drive excellent results. Everyone is kept to a higher standard and thus the results are significantly higher than individual effort. Graduate level programs learned this long ago and classes are broken down into work and study groups. No one wants to be considered an underachiever or to be holding back the group.

Division of labor also saves time. You can accomplish so much more with great effectiveness and diversity. Sometimes speed can make all the difference.

Seek out and become part of a great team. Volunteer for a committee at work. Watch and study the dynamics. Learn the positives and negatives. A good leader can spot when someone has a good idea but is hesitant to bring it up.

I've also found that brainstorming can really help here. This was especially effective in London with the British. The British have a tendency to really respect authority and don't want to appear stupid, or rather, non-intellectual. Being the leader and floating "dumb" or "silly" ideas really helps break down those barriers. In addition, some of the craziest ideas have affected a new line of thinking within the group and can lead to some very interesting approaches. I've seen some amazing things happen with this kind of exercise.

Set goals; no one can predict to what heights you can sore, even you will not know until you spread your wings.
—Unknown

Learning can only happen in a non-threatening environment.
—Unknown

Government has been a fossil: it should be a plant.
—Unknown

Never tell people how to do things. Tell them what to do and they will surprise you with their ingenuity.
—George S. Patton

If you really want to be up in life, look for the good in other people and tell them about it.
—Unknown

Don't point a finger, lend a hand.
—Unknown

Helping others is what helps ourselves.
—Unknown

As the greatest achievements were at first and for a time dreams. The oak sleeps in the acorn.
—James Allen

If you want a kinder world, then behave with kindness; if you want a peaceful world, reach within.
—Dan Millman

There are two ways of exerting one's strength; one is pushing down, the other is pulling up.
—Booker T. Washington

Have faith in people. Cynicism sours the disposition.
—Abraham L. Feinberg

No matter what accomplishments you make, somebody helped you.
—Althea Gibson

People put invisible leashes on themselves.
—Unknown

EMPOWER EVERYONE

So many people really don't know how good they are or can be. Guiding people, versus telling them what to do, for example suggesting a particular direction is a huge difference. When people are empowered, they are strong. They act differently; they walk differently. I had a lot of fun watching people who were talented but held back by the actions of a tough supervisor finally break out and fly.

People hold themselves back. I don't know why, but they often do. I believe it gets back to our earlier topics of belief or confidence and fear of failure or success. People put invisible leashes on themselves. As a leader, your job is to take those leashes off and let them run. If they are good, they will fly. I often talk about great people being like thoroughbred horses. You must let them run and not hold them back. So much of American business management intentionally holds people back. What an incredible waste. All this waste of time and effort, all in the name of control or trying to look good or not having someone else look better. Imagine the productivity if this didn't exist! It doesn't have to exist, under your control. Don't fall into that trap. Helping people doesn't make you look weak; it makes you strong. Harry Truman once said, "You can accomplish anything, if you don't mind who gets credit for it." What a powerful statement.

Just like in *It's a Wonderful Life*, people simply don't realize what they can do or what they have already done to contribute or be successful. George Bailey empowered an entire community by doing the right thing and he didn't even realize it. When he got a view of what the world would have been like without him, he still had a hard time seeing it. We have so much effect on the people around us; why not make it even more by empowering the people around you. They won't have any idea what you are doing to help them, but that isn't the point. The point is to help people. Understanding how you effect and help people is your reward and can change your life at the same time. The success and freedom they feel will have a "George Bailey" effect on people they touch as well.

You don't have to recreate the wheel, greatness is around you.
—Unknown

I always turn to the sports page first, which records people's accomplishments. The front page has noting but man's failures.
—Unknown

Hitch your wagon to a star.
—Ralph Waldo Emerson

Think and act like an industry leader.
—Unknown

Read and identify with successful people.
—Unknown

Don't copy something you can't imitate.
—Unknown

Success begets success.
—Unknown

Successful people have learned from their mistakes, join in.
—Unknown

Habits change into character.
—Ovid

I have studied the lives of great mean and famous women, and I found that the men and women who got to the top were those who did the jobs they had in hand, with everything they had of energy and enthusiasm.
—Harry S. Truman

Like it or not—you are a model. And, you're a parent; you are your children's first and foremost model. In fact, "you cannot not model." It's impossible. People will see your example—positive or negative—as a pattern for the way you believe life is to be lived.
—Unknown

A candle loses nothing by lighting another candle.
—Chinese Proverb

All personal breakthroughs begin with a change in beliefs.
—Anthony Robbins

To acquire knowledge, one must study; to acquire wisdom, one must observe.
—Marilyn vos Savant

MODELING

I am a great believer in this concept. Modeling has had an enormous affect on my decision-making, my approaches to problem solving and my approach to various business situations. There are so many brilliant people in this world. Learning the best or most successful traits is a very smart and effective way of improving your own skill set.

If you have someone you truly respect, think about why you respect them and decide if he or she is the right model for you. In my past, I very carefully studied the way people I respected handled a negotiation situation. I tried to conduct a thorough debrief, after the fact, to see and question why they did or said something in the meeting. Having a master explain his strategy gave me an education by the finest people in their field in the world. It sometimes took guts to ask the questions, however. Over time, I remember instances when I would see what the person was doing and predict what he would say next. I then developed those skills and started thinking like the "teacher" or CEO. I would also see the views of others in the meetings that I led. I wanted to know what was happening around me, as well as people's reactions to various topics or ideas. In addition, I would ask their opinion of my approach. They then started noticing what I wanted, and then I could rely on their work in my absence. It bred success.

Brad Nebergall, one of my best friends and a good person, once made fun of me and taught me a valuable lesson. We were in London on assignment together and we had just finished a quarterly business review (QBR) with Rich Kinder, Enron's former president and COO. Rich had very distinct mannerisms in his approach, thought process, voice and body language. He also chomped on an unlit cigar. We had finished the QBR and Brad commented to me to stop acting like Kinder. He pointed out that I was talking and doing hand motions just like him. That fact stunned me, although I was a big modeler and Rich was someone I respected tremendously. I had done it so often and unconsciously that I carried it on without noticing. There were times when I really did begin thinking and approaching business with his point of view. Wow, thinking like a captain of industry as a young vice president! What an advantage this was for me. I did this with many others as well.

People have bad habits, too. No one is perfect and so many have—I guess everyone has—a dark side. If you are modeling yourself after someone you really respect, remember that doesn't have to mean modeling everything. Pay attention to this. Maybe if you pick up the really strong and outstanding characteristics you can actually improve the original version!

Take an action step on this. Ask yourself whom do you really respect and want to model. Make a list of people you respect, and pick up the phone and meet with them. See if they have time for a cup of coffee or lunch. You would be surprised how many people will be receptive to the approach. If you are open about what you want to talk to them about and that you need some advice from them, many will make some time for you. I am a mixture of many successful people, like my father, Ken Lay, Ron Burns and so many more that it is impossible to list. Begin the process now.

Chapter Eight:

Office Politics

This is a dangerous and ugly topic. Every company has office politics. It isn't a very pretty part of a company. It is something that you will have to deal with. I am a believer that you don't have to play politics. You don't have to play but that doesn't mean you don't have to pay attention to what is going on. That is extremely important. In addition, you should pay attention to what your superiors expect. I don't think trying to do a good job and giving leaders what they expect is playing politics or being a "brown nose."

When someone asks you about a project, decision or philosophy, think about what the question really is. It may be asking for a simple clarification or real interest or it may include other issues or fears embedded within the question. Pay attention to where the asker is going, especially if he is going in a direction that doesn't make sense or may illustrate a lack of real understanding or communication. Many times people avoid confrontation by asking questions to get to the same place. Do pay attention also to politically minded people that may not have your interests in mind. Ask yourself, "Why are they asking about it?" As I have stated earlier, you don't have to play political games at work but you must pay attention to those who do.

The key is to do what is right and work very hard. Keeping your boss informed at all times and being enthusiastic about your job or assignment may come across again as being a "brown nose." This just isn't true if your intent is not to make yourself look good but is genuine about sharing the progress and doing a good job and passing on the results or progress. Your boss will know the difference. Besides, results speak for themselves. That will differentiate you from people who are jealous or simply trying to prop themselves up.

DEALING WITH YOUR BOSS

Know your boss and organization. You must pay attention to what your boss or superior wants or expects from you and the staff. This isn't attempting to be a brown nose but simply trying to do a good job and trusting that he knows what he wants. Remember he may just have a reason for wanting it that way. It could also be a simple matter of survival. If your boss has a peculiar or important "principle" why not follow his lead or need? It just makes sense. Here is a simple example: If your boss hates being late or starting meetings late, simply don't be late, period. Common sense is the key here. Just be smart about it. If being on time really bothers you, don't fight it, get over it or leave. Try having a little trust in your boss. He is there for a reason and you might just learn something from him or her even if there are some things you really don't like or don't fit your personality. Modeling your behavior on his or her successful traits might really help. It will certainly make your life easier.

Talk your boss up and help him. I have always been a believer that if you help your boss look good, he or she will treat you well. I have lived that good fortune for a long time. Again, this is simply being a good employee and friend. Your boss must trust you. If he does, then you'll do well and be more successful. Treat your boss with respect. Make sure that you don't have some agenda, and that talking him or her up to his superior is genuine. If you don't care for your boss and don't look up to them, don't stab them in the back or be unsupportive. It is your obligation to inform his superiors of serious issues or you have the obligation to move on. Don't be a bad person, even if your boss doesn't deserve your admiration or support. Again, you can always leave. Don't take this opportunity to put him down even if the chance is there. There certainly will be opportunities but you must have the discipline not to take the shot. There will be times that you really want to, but you must contain yourself.

Tell your boss when you meet with his superiors. I also developed a habit that endeared me to my many bosses over the years. When I would meet with one of his superiors, whether in the hallway or at a formal meeting, I would be religious about picking up the phone or stopping by and letting my boss know that we had met. I don't recall a time when I didn't inform my boss when I talked with one of his superiors whether it was a meeting, chance encounter or when asked to leave an update on voicemail. In fact, usually when I left an update to a senior manager, I would record it if possible, send it to the person and send a copy to my boss at the same time. If I couldn't do that, I consistently made sure that I immediately sent my boss an update and voicemail as soon as I hung up the phone. I was very disciplined about it. They realized that I didn't have any ulterior motives and that I didn't let the boss surprise them with a question that they didn't know how to answer.

I think this is very important with my people. I always tried to encourage or especially not discourage communication with senior people, but I did want to know what they had said so that I would not be out of the loop if asked. You can learn very quickly an employee's intention and motivation, and by the way, you never forget. I have made it a habit to encourage people to meet with my superiors or bosses. I think it builds confidence and a better work force. All I ask is that they leave me a voicemail, so I am in the loop.

DON'T GOSSIP

I addressed this in other sections but the lesson is valuable. Just don't do it. If you find yourself in a situation where you stated something that turned out to be false, incorrect or unfair, make the call and apologize and set the record straight as fast as you can. You certainly won't want to do it and you may put it off, but the damage will mushroom. Admitting you were wrong and correcting yourself can save a lot of pain for everyone involved.

DON'T BAD-MOUTH ANYONE

No matter how tempted you are—and boy will you be tempted—don't do it. As a rule, just assume that no matter whom you are telling, no matter how deep a secret it is, it will get out. If you care whether the person you are talking about were to hear it, then don't say it. I have not always followed my advice but even as I write this now, I wish I had. It is so easy to want to gossip, but you must resist the temptation. I didn't gossip many times, but sometimes I did slip or pass on information too quickly without verifying it. You will learn quickly when you do pass on bad or mistaken information just how difficult it is to take it back and make sure that you don't become part of the misinformation flow. You will also find out just how fast people pass on that type of information.

TAKE PEOPLE OUT TO LUNCH

One practice that I have found had a big influence on my work life was taking people out to lunch to get to know them better. If you work with someone and interact with him or her, I think it can be very effective to get out of the office and get know him or her a lot better. It improves your effectiveness when you have more than quick meetings and serious conversations. When I was president of Houston Pipe Line (HPL) and was on the management committee for Enron Capital & Trade, our wholesale group, our chief information officer was Philippe Bibi. We never interacted except for sitting at the same table in weekly staff meetings. I called him one day and scheduled a lunch. I had no real agenda other than just to get to know him better and for us to update each other on our jobs. It was a very nice lunch and we bonded. A year later, Jeff Skilling asked me (rather told me) to take over technology for the company and Philippe became a direct report. He was very upset at the decision but came around and didn't leave the company because he knew me from that lunch. When you have lunches or interactions without a purpose, it pays dividends. In addition, the walls were down and we came to know each other as people and peers rather than competitors. Although it took a while, we ended up being good friends and got along very well in the technology business. I ended up promoting him to chief technology officer for the entire company rather than CIO of one business unit. In an aggressive business environment, everyone assumes you have some agenda and you only call when you need something.

Also, if you do have reasons to go out with someone, call them for lunch on occasion when you don't need to talk about something. Especially something that may be of conflict. Have a long-term relationship that doesn't depend on getting together and having dialog only when it serves your interest.

DON'T ALWAYS SIT AT THE HEAD OF THE TABLE

This is something else that I don't always practice, but I preach. It is good idea, though. People know who is running the meeting or in command of the situation. You don't always have to prove it by making the point. In staff meetings, try getting there early and moving around the table. You can also learn something interesting by watching where everyone sits when you do move around. Round tables take care of this situation. I usually have a round table in my office and it takes away the issue. A true leader does not have to exercise his or her authority.

DON'T DO SOMETHING STUPID

When you do, learn from it and don't ever repeat it.

There will be times that you will be very tempted to gossip, listen and contribute to rumors or say something you shouldn't to be funny or simply because you are mad or feel cheated. Resist. Resist with all your might. I have given into temptation many times. You know immediately because as soon as you say it you know you shouldn't have. Making the mistake is inevitable but at least try to limit it. Never talk about something confidential, comment about a person, project or a rumor in an elevator or bathroom. I have overheard many bad things in both places. This includes all public places even if, actually especially, if they appear to be empty or okay. When you let your guard down you will get in trouble. You can't take back things said in that type of venue.

I was on the receiving end of this once and it made a profound difference on my huge project in London. I was leading a team to solve the J-Block take or pay problem in London and one of my analysts overheard two people on an airplane traveling to the US, seated near two British Gas employees. They were talking about Enron, the J-Block issue and BG's approach. They actually talked about the negotiations; how BG was stringing us along and would never settle but would keep us on the hook until they ran Enron into the ground and got us out of the UK and Europe. When the analyst reported to me upon landing, it changed our entire strategy and had a huge impact on reaching a settlement in the end. There was another lesson learned that day. It wasn't a positive one but truly illustrated the "dirty pool" that some people would play in business. That conversation, overheard on an airplane, cost their company hundreds of millions of dollars and maybe even a great deal more. It affected our family and helped in solving one of the most difficult business issues in the world.

E-mail is the most dangerous of all communication tools. I remember a situation in 1996 that almost cost me my career. I was in London working on the J-Block assignment when an e-mail came out to all employees about Enron's stock price, including an explanation of its current stock stagnation. It was a good communication and addressed two primary problems that were holding the company back. They were the issues surrounding the Portland General merger and the J-Block take-or-pay issue. I got the e-mail late one night in our Park Street office and sent a response to Geoff Roberts, my old boss and good friend, stating that we were to blame and must save the company. It was humorous but also had a bite to it. Instead of sending it to him as a "forward," I accidentally clicked "reply all" and sent it as a response back to the office of the Chairman and to all employees. We had 10,000! As soon as I hit the button and it came up as "send" my body went stiff, my pulse quickened, a pit swelled in my stomach, which felt like it was to be followed by vomiting. Sweat instantly began to appear on my forehead. How could I tell my wife about this? How do I explain this to people? How could I have destroyed my career so easily? All these thoughts flew through my mind. Writing about it now actually gives me a horrible pit in my stomach all over again. After about five seconds had passed, and my life had flashed before my eyes, a message came back, stating that I couldn't send a message back to a global e-mail. I almost fell out of my chair in relief. I had a second chance to live and vowed I would never make that mistake again, ever. A very valuable lessoned learned. It was a true gift.

Chapter Nine:

Learning

KNOW YOUR WEAKNESSES

Pick the weeds in your garden.
—Denis Waitley

The financial side of the business, including income statements, balance sheets and cash flows, was not my strength. In fact, I had had very little exposure since business school, 20 years ago. I needed to have a better understanding before I could be a good company president. It was very important. I informed my boss of my issue and told him of my enrollment in the University of Chicago executive course in finance. Chicago was recognized as having the finest finance school in the country. Completing the course helped me a lot and filled a huge gap in my knowledge. Years later, I still don't consider finance strength, and I could really use a refresher; but the course rounded me out as an executive.

You can't be good at everything, but you don't have to be bad either. Some management philosophies think differently about this. I read one book that even went so far as to state that you shouldn't even try to improve because you will be spending time to be mediocre at something, when you could have invested that time at improving and making a strength even better. I don't agree with that philosophy. Being poor at something can't be a positive. This philosophy is too clever for itself.

One big personal experience that had a dramatic effect on my life was Toastmasters. I was a good speaker or presenter in the mid 1980s but that suddenly changed. As a young businessman in 1986, I was making a presentation to the vice president of Exploration as a landman at Champlin Petroleum Company, and I had a terrible experience. My exploration manager, Del Bass, a great person and a great exploration & production guy, had asked me to present all the

149

progress I had in a farm-out program in the Appalachian area. I had great success and we were making a bunch of money because of my efforts and initiative. It remains today as one of my big successes in my career.

While presenting the maps with the wells and successes, a tough VP got furious about the fact that he had instructed my boss to dump the acreage and began verbally raking him over the coals. I simply stood up there while his boss crushed him. Within two weeks, I transferred into a new region. It taught me a couple of things, including how not to make stupid business decisions. That event affected me for years. That executive made a very bad call for the sake of control. He also should have never made such a public display by lambasting one of his top people. He could have and should have done that privately, certainly not in front of a lot of junior people in his group, like me. He was a bad manager. After that event, I then got nervous every time I had to present and it got worse and worse.

Finally, later that year, I read a prayer at my sister Anne's wedding and I was so nervous that I barely got through it. That was enough. I realized that day that if I didn't change my ways, it would hold me back for the rest of my work life. I then read about Toastmasters at work and bravely showed up one morning and joined in. It was great and had a profound effect on me. I was terrified, especially at first, but I regained my confidence and became an outstanding speaker. Years later, I was even paid $15,000 to be a speaker at conference. I picked the weed in my garden and if I hadn't, our lives would be much different today. That event and choice changed our lives and the lives of my children.

HIRE AN EXPERT

What separates those who achieve from those who do not is in direct proportion to one's ability to ask others for help.
—Donald Keough

When you are a manager and you see an issue with your work, get help. If you can, hire someone on your team to fill in the gap. It will be a great opportunity to work with someone who can help and be a valuable part of the team. If he or she is a complement to the team, the team is more powerful. I have some weaknesses on the financial side. I've never worked in that arena and I've always surrounded myself with people I could trust and experts to fill those important jobs. Everyone wins here, and you learn a lot about an area that you don't really know. It is important to know what you don't know.

It is also important to hire an expert when you are looking for help, not just because you have a weakness. I often used McKinsey and Company for strategy help at Enron. Enron used them all the time; in fact, we spent many millions of dollars a year on them. I joined in and found their help to be insightful and a way to sharpen the focus and move a business forward quickly. Consultants like McKinsey were also very helpful with internal politics. They usually liked what we were doing and reported back to Jeff Skilling and others what great things we were doing and validated a great deal of our efforts. That support helped us a lot when we went for approvals of projects or new businesses.

There is tremendous value in educating yourself in an area of weakness, but remember that you don't have to be the expert all the time. Bringing in the right person or team will allow you to focus on what you do best.

TRY SOMETHING DIFFERENT

Failure is merely feedback.

If something isn't working, change your approach. You certainly know what isn't working so why keep trying it? Change. Change it big. Shake it up and shake out the cobwebs. When you are really stuck, throw the cards up in the air and see what pops out.

Don't give up on the hard or difficult task. Just try something different. Each time you take a different approach you learn something that will help you complete whatever you are working on. I love shaking things up and seeing a new direction or where a new approach takes you. When I used to get really stuck on the J-Block project in London, I would walk to the Tate museum and walk around to clear my head. I would look at new approaches in art. Looking at a Matisse or Picasso that was created 70 years ago and was wild, absolutely wild for its time, helped me think of different approaches and unleash creativity that was stuck inside and constrained by the day-to-day activities or influenced by traditional business viewpoints. I had to break out of that way of thinking in order to solve the problem.

To help you accomplish this, talk to others or new people to get a fresh perspective. You may really need to look at the situation through someone else's eyes. The danger with having a lot of experience in a particular area is that you could become stagnant. Albert Einstein once made some comments about physics that are relevant here. He shared a view that a genius physicist must have a discovery by the time he turned 29 years old because after that, his opportunity for original thought was seriously diminished. Although I find that hard to believe in a strict sense, there is a lot of philosophical truth to it. One of the reasons that I believe I have been successful is that I did have many different positions and therefore brought new, "fresh" perspectives to various jobs. As you move through life and various jobs, I think that is worth considering. If you find yourself very comfortable in a job, maybe it is time to switch areas, force yourself into new and uncharted waters before you turn 29 but have many 29th birthdays in your life.

BUILD A SUPPORT SYSTEM

This has paid dividends repeatedly. I don't just mean that it is some political game to play with intrigue. It does mean, though, that you build trust and a support system to help you do your job better, test ideas, discuss things and of course manage your possible enemies. I believe in an organization, a person gets jobs, promotions or larger bonuses because of the small things or table conversations that people have about you. In a tie, do the spoils go to the nice person or the ruthless one? Positive or negative; team player or cowboy; popular or isolated; known or unknown? What do you think? People want to support good, hardworking people. I believe that when my bosses would occasionally go for the promotion or the bigger bonus or option grant, my actions and personality helped in more ways than I ever knew. It is still about how you live or the kind of person you really are, but having the broad support system also plays an important role.

YOU CAN LEARN SOMETHING FROM EVERYONE

Listen respectfully to each person.

Learning is living. You should pay attention to lessons that you can learn in everyday life and from anyone at any time. Learning even the small things can have an effect. You must have the attitude that you can learn from everyone and if you believe that, you have a healthy attitude on life. I think this also relates to respect. If you respect everyone and realize that every human being has value, then you can see the opportunity within him or her.

Chapter Ten:

Feedback

WHEN GIVEN FEEDBACK, LISTEN AND DON'T DISMISS

When someone gives you feedback or advice, listen. That doesn't mean that you must believe it or that you must follow it, simply that you should listen. Don't dismiss things out of hand, especially if they are negative. Opinions may be wrong or don't take into account all the facts—but not every time. Listen and hear what others are saying. Very often, some truth or issue may have merit. The expression, "Perception becomes reality" applies here. Sometimes what you think you are doing and how you are actually acting or behaving may be different. You may be so focused or busy that you've lost your way a little and need redirection. Even if a little. We had some training in 1997 called Executive Impact. This had some 360-degree feedback and the confidential comments back on my performance were very insightful and interesting. Often I was actually attempting to act a particular way with an individual but when I saw its interpretation in writing, it made me ponder my actions and reconsider. Usually I consciously made the decision not to change what I was doing but at least it was a decision, and I listened.

LEARN FROM YOUR MISTAKES

I didn't fail 100 times; I learned something on each of my previous 99 attempts.
—Thomas Edison

Learning from your mistakes is vital. You have to pay attention.

153

Failure is truly feedback. If you can really believe that, your life will be much easier. People make mistakes all the time and unfortunately, they will never stop. The key is to move on. Many people freeze in place from fear of making a mistake. Most people want to be right or even perfect. They will be very disappointed and not succeed or grow. Learning leads to growth; take advantage of every opportunity.

RECOGNITION

Everyone wants to be recognized and appreciated.

Everyone wants to be recognized for excellent results and hard work. So many senior managers underestimate the importance of this, and it is a serious issue. Many believe that the "warm and fuzzies" aren't important and that doing a good job is a requirement so why praise people for earning their paycheck. They are so wrong. Money doesn't drive people—accomplishment and job satisfaction do. Study Maslow's *Hierarchy of Needs*, and you will see this in plain black and white. Maslow argued that, as we meet our basic needs, we strive to satisfy higher needs. Basic needs would include food, water, security, and friendship; higher needs would be morality, creativity, spontaneity, among others. Many studies have proven that a raise or bonus affects people for very short periods only. The best employees perceive work as fun and feel appreciated. They must not feel they are simply performing a function.

Recognizing people in groups is also a grossly underestimated key to success. If someone has done something great, tell him or her you appreciate it and recognize it. Written notes are great, and you should use these, but not in place of verbal praise. I really enjoy watching people swell with pride when they earn recognition and get it. The dividends of this action pay very well. Don't take this to mean, however, that you should do it falsely or just to do it. False or insincere praise will damage your credibility with everyone. It will mean nothing, and it will cause people to doubt your sincerity on everything.

Written notes are very important. People will keep them. I have one friend and employee named Jim, an accounting and finance person, who had some great accomplishments for which I wrote him a note thanking him for his outstanding work. Years later when he was showing off some of his prized deal toys for closing big transactions, I saw my handwritten note of appreciation inside the trophy. I've even seen them displayed in other places. I have done the same. I've kept many notes from bosses going back over 20 years! Think about that; notes from 20 years ago! Do you think there is power in this?!

PERFORMANCE REVIEWS

Always conduct performance reviews on your employees. Really do them. I can't say that I ever enjoyed spending the time it took to do a thorough performance review but I can say that it paid huge dividends. Spending the time to talk about someone's performance not only helps the person know where you stand but it shows him or her how much you really care. So many people don't understand this, and I actually mean almost every single person I know in senior management. Use the system you have in place in the company. I did very complete and lengthy reviews on all my managing directors and most of them were stunned and told me that they hadn't had any type of feedback much less a written review in years. It certainly wasn't always pleasant but they all really appreciated it. It will pay off for you.

Another tool that helped me a lot was the self-assessment. I had to do one on myself early in my career and I used it for many years. I asked my employees to do them on themselves, it was very insightful and I was able to save time by using much of what they had to say about themselves in their reviews. In addition, they are often harder on themselves than I would be.

If you want to know where to focus on improvement, I would do one on yourself even if it isn't required. You don't have to give it to anyone but you can see very quickly the areas that you need to work on and specifically where you are doing well. At the very least, it will make you more prepared for the review you will receive from your boss. It is hard for a boss to tear you up on an area in which you are not strong if you have already identified what it is and taken action steps to improve. You can turn a developmental need or weakness into a positive, immediately.

Pay attention to the items on the review. There may be a reason why those items were included to begin with. They also illustrate what the company stands for and what they value. How do you fit with what the company is looking for? What does the "ideal" or number one rated employee act and look like? What are the skills required to be the best in your field? It is very hard for a company, even in the hardest of economic times, to let go of the best.

Conducting performance reviews is good for your employees, but it can also help you improve, as well. That's something to consider.

Don't Sip Your Own Whiskey

Enjoy applause but never quite believe it.
—Various

One of my personality traits that really helped me be successful is my passion for what I am doing. My wife would say that I am compulsive or have an addictive personality. She may be right. I can become very excited about things and run off in a new direction or business. Again, this is one of the reasons that I am successful in the business world. But, it is also a trait to be aware of, and I have always done so. I always take an idea and talk about it with some of my trusted and smart peers or friends. I think it is good to do this in all stages, but there is a danger of doing it before you thoroughly consider most of the items. You must be able to trust these peers and friends. If you "test" yourself or an idea occasionally, it makes sure that you don't sip your own whisky. One word of caution however, just because someone else doesn't like an idea or viewpoint doesn't mean you shouldn't pursue it. It means you think about what the person said as input. It is still your choice to accept or reject it. The real key is if several or many people share the same view. This is like asking your friends about your girlfriend; if they all dislike like her, watch out. They are seeing something you don't. Just don't ignore others' views out of hand and especially take care not to believe that you don't need others' input!

One other thing to remember: Enjoy the afterglow of doing a great thing or reaching some big benchmark but don't let it go to your head. Enjoy it because there will be bad times as well. Don't believe your own press.

Have Fun and Enjoy Your Successes

You must enjoy the successes life gives you when you get them. It is not a game, with winning the game being the only outcome. Winning is very sweet and brings you the satisfaction you desire. But, there are a thousand steps in that journey—not just the end. Many of those steps will be bad as well. Very bad. You must enjoy making headway and celebrate progress. Most positions don't provide instant gratification, there will be many peaks and valleys. Yes, the valleys come in any situation and they can hit you hard. If you don't enjoy the peaks, the valleys will seem much worse than they actually are. Many people take the hard times so hard, including me, but if you never recognize and take pleasure in the good times, it will be so much harder to get through those periods. Remember those times and use them to keep plugging away when you feel like giving up.

Section 3—Negotiations

The J-Block Negotiation

It is funny how things work when you write a book. I've attempted to document all the things that contributed to making me a successful person. My work assignments have had one key element in common: They all centered on being a deal maker. All kinds of deals and negotiated transactions and it all began with my very first professional job in 1983. Little did I realize that starting out as a petroleum landman would lead to such a long deal-making journey. As I have reviewed in other parts of the book, you must really enjoy what you are doing to be good at your job. In fact, I should say "great" rather than "good." You want to be great at what you're doing. Enjoyment and success are definitely linked. They are part of the cybernetic loop. I simply love putting deals together.

I do want to touch on a couple of important pieces of deal making. First of all, it really gets down to having strong people skills. Reading people, thinking about things from the other person's perspective, and listening are all very important to a successful conclusion, whether it is about a long, drawn-out ugly negotiation or simply agreeing on contract terms that fit both company's needs. The reality is that there is a combination of many topics in this book that lead to being a successful dealmaker. I believe that one of the keys to a successful negotiation is the level of preparation you put into it. There is a very direct correlation of hard work to success. This is vital, unless your counterpart is simply incompetent. You just can't fake being completely prepared and over-thinking the situation. Going over your proposal, rehearsing your negotiations, thinking about responses to areas in which your position is weak; all are vital to the successful outcome. Do it again then do it one more time. You must outwork your opponent and, most of all, don't ever underestimate him or her. Even if it doesn't appear to be the case, he or she is good and is your counterpart for a reason. The counterpart is working hard and is passionate for their side of the deal. You don't have to live in the land of complete paranoia about their strategy, but you must assume that they are working just as hard on their side as you are working on yours.

What is your driver for getting the deal done? The very minute you think, "If I get this deal closed I'll earn a bonus," your deal is in real jeopardy. I'm not trying to be unrealistic here. Of course when you are closing commercial transactions it is natural to think about the consequences of your potential success, but you must squash those thoughts. You have to close the deal because it is the right thing to do and the best thing for the company, not because it is best for you. Bonuses, recognition, and promotions come as a consequence to your success and should never be the driver of your purpose. The focus on personal gain affects every decision from that point forward in the course of the negotiation. Making personal decisions can lead you down a very different path, resulting in bad decision-making, thus failure. A recent situation at Jones Energy comes to mind. We were going through a sales process, and everything in the marketplace was going against us, so much so that it is almost laughable (almost). Our sales price kept getting lower and lower due to the drop in natural gas prices, and we were at our very limit, struggling over what decision to make. We were very close to making a deal, but both Jonny Jones and I were struggling with the call. I sat back one evening, actually in the middle of the night, and thought of the financial consequences of not making the sale. Managing the company's debt and limiting potential opportunities were plaguing me. There was also a very direct personal gain for many people at the company. It meant a very serious financial payday for many of our top employees and of course it meant many millions and millions of dollars to the McConnell and Jones families. As much as I thought it all through, the money was just one component of the decision and it was not the driving force. You only really know that in the middle of the night when it is just about you and your thoughts. We did not complete the transaction and, although one never knows what the best outcome really is at the time, we believe we made the right call.

There are excellent books and seminars on the art of negotiation. I strongly suggest you read some of those books and invest your time and money actually to go through a class. The results will assist you for the rest of your life. I also make it a habit to keep my favorite negotiation resource in my office and, when I am entering a negotiation, I scan the chapters and remind myself of the entire process especially attempting to see where the other party is going. One expression stands out and I think about all the time: "A tactic known is no tactic at all."

As I review all the different types of deals and work that I have done, I realize they are too numerous to present as a summary. Instead, I have decided to share one significant transaction from start to finish. That negotiation is known as "J-Block." It was infamous around Enron and was significantly covered by the press in Europe. Except for actual news updates on court decisions or the media coverage upon the final outcome, it was brought up in only one significant write up during the process in the US. *Forbes Magazine* came out with an article in the

March 11, 1996 edition and it brought out its seriousness and effects on the company. I must admit it was fun, although nerve-wracking, to see something you are doing written up in a magazine, especially as a young vice president.

Here is my one real example. I hope this gives you a general picture of negotiating a big transaction and how we approached the situation.

TAKING THE RISK

In my life, I've been part of some of the most interesting negotiations a person can experience. I've had the pressure of the world, at least our work world, on me and found out I could take it. Not only could I take it, but also I was able to lead the task to the end with a successful conclusion. One such negotiation was the J-Block project. I knew it was a tough assignment, but even so, I had no idea that I was walking into a transaction that would affect all gas deals in the North Sea, be the biggest company issue at Enron, deal with geopolitics, have our home and office swept for listening devices (bugs) in a worry of corporate espionage and be written about in *Forbes Magazine*.

The first challenge I faced was that my new job was in London, England. I had just finished the Florida Power & Light negotiations the year before and had begun to get a reputation as a major "deal guy." However, I wondered, was it really me or was it Geoff Roberts, my boss? We did a great deal of the negotiations together and he was simply outstanding. I learned so much from him. I don't think we could have done the deal without him. But, even if Geoff was the main catalyst or reason for getting the deal closed, I did go through the experience and learn how he did it, and now it was part of my skill set and my business prowess. I used modeling to get a good grasp of Geoff's approach and thought process. "I can do this," I said to myself, though I was nervous. I later thought, "Thank goodness I had no idea what was really in store with this project."

In the summer of 1994, Geoff approached me to join him in London and help change Enron's presence in Europe. We were dear friends and we trusted each other implicitly. After the successful deal with FP&L, the company promoted him, he took the job as CEO of Enron Europe and moved to England. He was to recreate the successful ECT model over in Europe. The company had done an extensive study of the opportunities in Europe but decided it was years away from true deregulation and expansion. In addition, Enron Europe had some ugly and large contract issues to deal with first. Geoff wanted me to fix those contract issues. We talked about the unique job experience and he asked me if I would join him and do FP&L one more time. The possibilities scared and intrigued me at the same time. On the day that Chris and our new child, Michael, came home from the hospital, I had to talk with her about the possibility. We had a cup of coffee and she listened intently as I described the position. A single tear fell from one eye. She knew this was something I really wanted to do, but more than that, it was something we were supposed to do.

I accepted the job that summer and everyone at work thought I was crazy, but I was off and commuting for several months. That arrangement lasted a great deal longer than anticipated due to housing issues. Chris and the kids stayed with her parents. It was a cramped time but it was great in that Chris' folks grew very close to their grandchildren, although that made it harder when I took them to London, which was very far away. My in-laws were unhappy with me.

In January of 1995, we finally moved the whole family to London. The challenges were upon us immediately. It rained every day for the first 61 days, and, with London getting dark at 3:30 p.m. that time of year, we never saw the sun. To make matters worse, Chris had to walk to get groceries every day all the way to the High Street at St. John's Wood with an infant and a three-year-old. We had a very nice, although very small, house in a great American neighborhood called St. John's Wood. It was incredibly expensive. The lease was $300,000/year! The company signed a contract for $1,000,000 just for our place to live. But, even with this, Chris wasn't very happy with our new life. Everything in London was different. Every brand of diaper, medicine and toothpaste—you name it. One nice change was having milk delivered to our door each day. Other than the milk, though, it was the worst six months of our marriage. But, we got through it together and began loving London.

We called the project simply "J-Block," in reference to a gas sales agreement Enron had made with the oil and gas producers to purchase all the gas from the Judy and Joann fields in the Central North Sea. The J-Block producers were an equal partnership of Phillips, BG and Agip with Phillips being the operator. They had spent $1 billion developing and finding a large amount of oil and gas. Early estimates showed reserves of 101 million barrels of oil and 1 Tcf of gas. Estimated production was 95,000 bbls/day of crude and 300 mmcf/d of gas. The gas was going to be transported via the Central Area Transportation System (CATS), which was owned by several companies and was operated by Amoco. Only the big boys played in this area of the world, and Enron had officially become one of the big boys. In the late 1980s, Enron successfully developed a huge, 1,800-megawatt power plant named Teesside. The gas cycle plant was one of the largest of its kind in the world and put Enron on the map as an international company.

However, to build the plant, they had to buy the feedstock—natural gas—from the North Sea. They did so successfully and had a good gas contract to feed a good power plant. The Everest and Lomond gas contract was very significant because it was a new, incremental contract for a growing new power business in a world of deregulation introduced by Margaret Thatcher.

Enron was convinced it could replicate this structure and began its power development growth strategy. The company began its work and had several power plant sites ready to go in England—almost ready to go. With impending closure, they had to negotiate buying the gas at the same time. This included buying long-term gas and transporting it to the power plant itself. They also had to do this in a natural gas environment dominated by the national gas company, British Gas. It was quite a task. It was also complicated by the lack of options to fit incremental plants and because BG never had buy and match supply and marketed in that fashion. It is nice to be a monopoly! The timing was such that Enron had to commit to the gas supply and transportation before the plant was finalized. Just as the contracts were committed, the regulatory changed in England and there was a moratorium on building new power plants in the UK. A problem was brewing, but it was years away and the gas contracts were put in a drawer to be addressed later while the company addressed more immediate issues. It was going to take years to find the gas and lay the pipeline. Time moved on and the day of reckoning for the gas contracts drew near.

A COMPLICATED CONTRACT

The J-Block gas contract was significant. It was a 15-year gas sales agreement. The obligation was firm, extremely firm, and it was a take-or-pay depletion contract. Take or pay means that Enron must take the gas or pay for it anyway as if it had been taken, and the contract then allowed making it up over time. These were firm contracts. The volume was enormous, with a minimum take obligation of 260,000 mcf/d with anticipated gas flows of the maximum of 300,000 mcf/d. That is a firm obligation to buy up to 1.4 Tcf of gas with a known fixed and escalating price and 100 percent of all the gas that can be produced. As time passed, deregulation of gas was occurring and a new pipeline was being potentially to potentially supply gas to the continent of Europe. Prices began to fall, and they fell like stone. Prices fell so low that this contract became the highest-priced contract in the North Sea. This translated into even more danger for Enron, because the price was so much better than any other, that the producers would have a super incentive to develop technologies or find ways to put the maximum amount of gas into our contract and not have any natural decline at all. The entire project was also very complex. The contract incorporated 11 major agreements and 130 related documents.

Enron, as the largest pipeline company in the United States, should have seen the risk coming. Amazingly, the UK and US office didn't communicate well. Especially when the UK office was all about power and the US was all about gas. Deregulation was just one factor in the puzzle. The size of the commitment was also a key that would have driven immediate action. The J-Block commitment was as much as five percent of all the gas moved in the UK and it was going to come online in one day when it was finally ready to flow. That is a lot of incremental gas to come on the market. More than that, it was incremental gas, with no home, to be "dumped" on the open market. You see, almost every other mcf had a market. This gas had no power plant and was going to become the entire market. In fact, it was approximately 50 percent of all gas on the market not committed to large market contracts. This was a formula for disaster. There was no home for this gas, at any price.

There was another huge complication. Enron had formed a company called Teesside Gas Transportation Limited (TGTL). It was a 50/50 joint venture with ICI (the big British chemical company). The partnership originally contracted for the transportation contract to move the gas from the fields onshore to the yet-to-be-developed power plant. That was a matching large send or pay contract for the full volumes. The Cats Reservation and Transportation Agreement (CRTA) had just as many issues and complications as the J-Block agreements. This agreement was even tighter than the take-or-pay agreement because Enron had to make the payments quarterly, not annually, if the volumes did not physically move. The timing of the contract commencement and payments didn't line up with the moving of the gas and there was a web of deception and game playing by the CATS parties. The transport fees were approximately .60/mmbtu; that equaled $15 million a quarter in fees. TGTL was paying that without moving any gas. There were huge issues with CATS, and just as I arrived, CATS had notified TGTL that the commencement date had occurred but they weren't ready to deliver the gas. They were exercising a very clever argument that TGTL had to start paying the transport fees upon the notification of the commencement date. The problem was that they weren't actually ready to commence deliveries. They claimed ability didn't matter, just notification. They were right about the language on the contract, but it clearly wasn't the intent. That is the problem with lawyers and contracts. We were using the same type of strategy along the way as a matter of survival.

They also had issues with delivery points. They had leaks in their interconnect, they had hydrocarbon dew point issues, they had high mercury levels in the gas specs and an inoperable receipt point. The quote "can't get the gas in and can't get the gas out" became our battle cry. The mercury issue became huge, and we were very focused on it. We discovered that they knew they were out of spec and very intentionally hid it from us. We would later learn in discovery and even on the stand in a court of law just how far they would go. They would lie to us; we watched people commit perjury! Writing it today still amazes me. The mercury issue was very serious, not just a contractual debate point. The gas was originally planned to feed a power plant with gas turbines. Those turbines have aluminum blades, and mercury is devastating to aluminum. We fought this with extreme passion. They were convinced we were just using it as an issue to get out of the obligation and we thought they didn't care at all about ruining power plants: They just wanted their money and would do anything to protect those cash flows. Both positions were certainly understandable.

BUILDING THE TEAM AND BRAINSTORMING

The issue came to a head when the CATS parties notified TGTL in November of 1994 of the official commencement date. It was clear they weren't actually ready to commence operations, so TGTL withheld the payment in the fourth quarter of 1994. The CATS parties sent another commencement date in March of 1995, just in case the court ruled their first commencement date insufficient. They upheld the legality of the first notice as well, of course. It was obvious that they were preparing their arguments for a lawsuit. They followed up in May with a lawsuit on TGTL. The battle began in the courts and would last, with intensity, for years.

I arrived in the late summer of 1994 and began working vigorously. I assembled a team and began to fight all the culture issues between Americans and the British. My first team member was Richard Harper. I was lucky because I inherited him as part of the project. He is a great person with a brilliant mind. He was the key to our eventual success and a tireless worker. We made a great team. We had so much to do, but neither of us had any clue of what was really about to happen to the company or to us. Another vital member of our team was Mary Nell Browning, our lawyer and a very special person. She had an amazing work ethic. She was a work machine and a dear friend. Her tireless dedication and partnership in this process made the ultimate negotiation a success.

Before the process even began, I was formulating thoughts about the negotiations, but I had yet to read all the thick contracts and understand not only the gas pieces but also all the subtleties of the North Sea and European ways of business.

As we were first beginning to form the team and our game plan, I took one very significant step that I still perform today: brainstorming the problem. I was one of the very first guests at a new modern hotel designed specifically for a business clientele. This was a novelty in the British hotel industry. One of the amenities provided by the hotel was a television with a built-in VCR, another new concept back then. I rented a couple of movies including *Gone with the Wind*. I worked during the entire movie and was glad it was very long. I sat with my laptop and brainstormed on the J-Block problem for hours while the scenes played. The brainstorming list was quite long and had many crazy ideas but some were very interesting and they led to other interesting variations on those ideas. That was the beginning of a "living" document of ideas that I would refer back to for the next couple of years.

The gas purchase agreement had so many issues. The price was very expensive, at one point about 3 times the market price; we had 100 percent take or pay; limited make up rights and the producers could keep putting in volumes as long as they could find gas. It seemed that almost every possible item was against Enron. Phillips and the original negotiator took such advantage of Enron's need that they "almost punished" them in the negotiations. At that time, Enron must have really wanted this gas supply, because not only was the price very high but also every paragraph in the agreements was in Phillips' favor. I was frustrated with the agreements. Not because we had committed to an above-market price (no one can predict years in advance what the future is going to hold) but because of the entirely one-sided terms. That would later come back to haunt the J-Block partners. I was able to use the extreme one-sidedness of the agreement to our advantage later. Not only would that later give us leverage, it would teach me a lesson that I would never forget about doing deals that are too one-sided.

That original brainstorming list was the basis of the first formal meeting we had with the head of the Phillips side of the table, Bill Van der Lee. Bill was known as the "king of gas" and was famous for taking Enron to the cleaners on the J-Block deal. Boy, did he take advantage of Enron! Bill was also Dutch, and the Dutch had a stereotype of being very tight and very tough. I don't know about the accuracy, much less the fairness of that stereotype, but it did fit Bill to a tee. In that first meeting, I distributed a refined list of my brainstorm ideas and everyone sat and stared at me. They thought I was crazy, bringing up all these different avenues of thoughts and possible directions for a solution. Bill did all the talking for Phillips in the meeting, and when I attempted to engage or even to look at others in his party, they would look at me, mystified, with mouths agape. They were shocked that I was addressing them and not Bill. They must have thought I was either very clever, attempting to get information, or just an idiot—probably the latter. My very American style kept them off balance, even when they believed it was some clever tactic. I really do believe they thought I was simply foolish.

That first meeting didn't go well at all, but I think it did set a tone that led them, over time, to believe that we were in a difficult situation and that we were at least attempting to find a fair solution. As difficult as this entire negotiation and project were, we always tried to find a solution that was good for everyone. I don't believe the J-Block group ever really believed that, but I do think in retrospect they may realize that I never lied to them. Enron was in a "life or death" fight, and to me that means you work as if everything is on the line, but you don't set morals or ethics aside. We had to find a solution, an answer. We examined every possible solution, but we never crossed the line. Sadly, I did find most of the J-Block team's tactics and issues to be very unethical. I believe they lied to me many times and that they felt okay about it because we were the "bad guys." As I am writing this, I am sure they felt the same way about us. It would be incredibly naïve of me to think they believed we were telling them the truth.

EXPOSURE

In May, discussions continued with a new lead negotiator, Steve Prendergrast. Steve was a very nice person, and Chris and I spent time with him and his wife and we liked them. I believe he worked hard to find a resolution. After extensive conversation and meetings, we put a proposal in front of Phillips on June 2. It was a good first proposal. We attempted to take the gas on a firm basis in various tranches of gas with various pricing. The six different pricing structures would insure that gas would flow from their perspective and provide us with degrees of "pricing pain" to make sure we didn't have to shut them in again, thus cutting off their oil or cash flows. It went beyond a contractual relationship, but to pricing that would be market based, thus insuring gas would physically flow. We had a significant amount based on an index price. Index was very innovative at the time and I don't believe any other contracts included this concept. It also introduced another concept: They could actually add more gas, or rather have delivery flexibility, for another block they were developing outside the GSA. It also gave them the ability to use our processing facilities for their gas. Again, it gave them the ability to manage their gas more effectively and be less "captive" to us. I thought it was a very good and innovative proposal. It would soon be rejected out-of-hand by Phillips management.

After a few months, the project moved forward again and with great progress; actually better than I could have dreamed. The real proof came when Rich Kinder and Ed Segner came to town for the quarterly business review (QBR) in June 1995. I was very nervous going into that meeting; my group had a special two-hour session with Rich and his staff. During the meeting, he learned for the first time that the problem may be in excess of $1.2 billion. That's $1,200,000,000 out of the money! However, I held my ground and reported the issues truthfully and with confidence. In the end, they loved the presentation and left with all the confidence in the world at the way we were handling the process. Rich even said later that he had never been so impressed with this type of a project in his entire tenure at Enron. Wow! I was still a victim of self-doubt and this proved to me that I really should listen to the people around me. I will never forget that week. I thought at the time, "That was fantastic; now, if I can just get the project done." I think he really understood just how good the team was.

The glow was short-lived, however. We issued an erroneous press release the one day I was out of the office. Rich Kinder called me three times at home for an update. This drove home (literally) the magnitude of my job and the size of the problem we faced. Although the press release caused a significant problem, it did give me one more opportunity to shine and we handled the situation perfectly.

September is usually a quiet month in Europe but not so for the J-Block team. The Enron Corp spotlight was turned back to London. Phillips Chairman Wayne Allen turned up the heat under J-Block again with a phone call to Ken Lay. A sudden meeting in London with each company bringing its respective president and COO followed the call. We spent two days briefing Rich Kinder and felt prepared for the big meeting. We wanted a permanent solution and were prepared to change the contract dramatically with a large cash payment ($100,000,000) as a starting position. The meeting went terribly and it ended after only a few hours with everyone taking a step backwards. Rich had a habit of chewing on an unlit cigar all the time, especially in meetings such as these. At the end, he bit right through it. It was a clash of the titans and the meeting taught me a lot about miscommunication and egos. The decision was that Enron was not going to take the J-Block natural gas for a couple of years. I was certain that would pay dividends later. We decided to issue a preemptive press release on the situation; we were just exercising our rights under the contract for the interests of our shareholders—not just being an aggressive party. Late into the night we drafted and revised the press release. It hit the wire at 8 a.m. the next morning, and, boy, did it pay off. Enron stock went up, and the NYSE did not allow Phillips stock to open, due to an imbalance of sell orders. We all hunkered down, reviewed press clippings and waited for the next big event. Phillips was furious and thought that we wrote the press release in advance and that the entire meeting was a sham. They couldn't believe we could work that fast. We would use that advantage repeatedly.

Rich Kinder's visit lasted and lasted. It was a difficult visit, to say the least. Having a president and COO hovering around was nerve-wracking, and on one occasion, I did a stellar job of sticking my foot in my mouth. While having drinks one evening, I mentioned that I had a Mercedes as a company car. Every expat had a Mercedes as a company car. Not only was having such a nice company car very controversial, but it also gave Kinder ammunition to nail me several times for the next few days. And boy did he use it. I used my ability to laugh at myself to turn it into a positive issue and used it as the spotlight on our relationship.

The exposure continued in the months ahead. In late September and then October, I negotiated private and confidential meetings with my counterparty from Agip. During numerous lunches, I fed him information and brought him up to speed with our point of view so he could discuss the situation with his partners. The plan was for him to raise these items as his own ideas. It is fair to say that this wasn't the normal way of negotiating a big deal. Ernest Sarpi was a good person and a true gentleman. We developed a strong bond and friendship. He understood that my intentions were honorable and that I really wanted to find a win/win solution to this huge problem. If not win/win at least not a lose/lose deal. We had many meetings and all were enjoyable. We commonly met at his favorite restaurant which just so happened to be the best Italian food in London. It was called Mimo's Discia and I can still taste it. I think Ernie enjoyed being my mentor, so to speak. I was not allowed to order off the menu and remember having to try fresh risotto that was pitch black due to the main ingredient being octopus ink.

It wasn't such a bad deal for me either. Dealing with Agip brought in another side benefit. Enron Chairman Ken Lay knew the chairman of ENI very well. Ken started calling me to get updates on the status of the negotiations. To borrow a risk management term, I was "long" on exposure at Enron. Ken came back to London several weeks later and we spent a long week going over everything in the transaction; it went better than expected. Being able to talk with Ken and all the executives helped me grow as a person and an executive. Very few people in the world got this kind of exposure at my level. It would change me forever.

November came with very little in the way of real progress. Enron's financial exposure kept increasing and increasing. The bench price for gas fell to $4.97 p/ therm, compared to the J-Block price of $18.50 p/therm. My God, how could it get any worse? Even as I recount this story, it staggers me. The personal exposure continued, including phone calls from Lay, many at home. The Enron team was ready for the battle royal when the gas was finally ready to flow until the time when the infrastructure was actually ready to take gas. Major lawsuits were ready for a November 26 deadline, when the facilities were scheduled and ready to go. If they actually flowed gas, whether to test it or sell it in a way that we are unaware of, they were to be served with writs on the GSA and the CRTA. We were in the headlines again. Only time would tell if they were to make such a bold move.

FEVER PITCH

1996 began with a bang regarding the J-Block project. We made quick and massive progress. Within two weeks, we made a final offer on January 23 and put $200,000,000 on the table to do the deal. It also limited the total amount of the total gas taken during the life of the agreement to 675 bcf. The pricing had several price tiers, providing us with incentives to take more gas. It also put a minimum take obligation of 130 mmcf/d, which gave them max oil flow. In addition, we gave them free transport on our CRTA contract to allow them to transport up to 130 mmcf/d on their own. If accepted, it would save us more than $1 billion! The approval process and preparation were amazing. Getting this much money and proposing this much pain to the organization was difficult. It was going to hurt the company a lot. Upon our final offer, there was no response for more than a week, and the silence was broken only because of an article in *Forbes* about Enron and J-Block, which forced a dialog and gave us a good indication of the progress that was taking place.

We actually waited more than six weeks for an answer after the *Forbes*-incited discussion and subsequent offer. The negotiation began with a visit to Bill's house, drinking coffee and discussing the outline of a deal and overall philosophies. Negotiating with the "king of gas" in his own house was a wild experience. His wife, who was very nice, served us coffee and biscuits on their formal china and then left us to do our business. In the end, we withdrew the offer and finally received a response that they were not interested in pursing it. It was unbelievable. Even Bill van der Lee from Phillips was stunned. He had always conceded that any offer and agreement were subject to board approval, but I believe he really expected this one to work. I was told later that he resigned over the handling of the deal. Apparently, he was not accustomed to being overruled when a deal was ready to go.

In March, Rich Kinder returned to London with the regular big regime, as well as Lou Pai. Lou was the president of ECT at the time and was known as a smart but difficult person. It was Lou's first visit and he was very tough and very prone to second-guess everything we had done so far. It was a terrible week that ended with a letter from Ken Lay, written by me, that was sent to the all the J-Block partner CEOs. Lord Wakeham, Rich Kinder and I went to speak to the Energy Minister, Tim Eggar. The formality of the meeting, the British way of discussion, the protocol, it was fascinating. These were very senior and well-known people. Spending a lot of time with a knight was very unique, what a great experience!

This was Rich's last visit to London. Within a couple of months, he would leave Enron due to a confrontation with the Board. Rich was to be Ken's successor but the Board extended Ken's contract, thus extending Rich's tenure as the number two guy at Enron. Rich and Ken made one of the best teams in corporate America. I had heard that Rich took the decision as an insult, the board not having the confidence that he could be the CEO versus the top COO in the business. He would soon leave, buy some unwanted assets from Enron, join a small company with an old friend of his, Bill Morgan, and form KinderMorgan, which would grow into an energy giant and make him a billionaire many times over. Rich is an amazing person; I learned so much by being around him. Ultimately, from a J-Block perspective it turned out to be a good thing, a good thing for the project anyway. No one could have predicted that in a few years Rich's decision to leave would lead to Jeff Skilling taking over and ultimately to a corporate scandal that would take down our great company and leave the name Enron synonymous with greed and corporate wrongdoing. Jeff Skilling would take over as president and COO which would prove to be a catalyst to action with Phillips.

The month of March continued with frenzy. In the last two weeks, we had to make huge decisions, the quick and massive buyout of ICI's ownership position, the first settlement proposal to the CATS parties and the possibility of terminating all the contracts. The last week of March was everything that was expected. While developing extremely complex legal arguments in the UK and the US, we had to buy out ICI in seven days. We were to offer them a fair deal but it was an interesting negotiation. We would pay nearly anything to get them out of the picture in our J-Block conflict and they would have done almost anything to get out of our developing battle as well. They realized that with the attitudes and global politics, the J-Block standoff was developing into the World War II of be business world. Peter Styles headed up the ICI negotiation and I had to play the role of the bad guy and senior executive. It was a very odd role and the negotiations were tedious and went over the tight deadline on Friday. At one point, I actually had to approve a wire of $100,000,000 without having an agreement in writing on the transaction. During that week, 16-hour days were the norm and every decision was enormous. We couldn't get ICI to finish the negotiations due to their "style" of negotiating. I was running out of time and the lead negotiator, a Brit who was on the board with me, was so painfully slow. It was as if he was being paid by the hour. We did have one trick up our sleeve. Our chairman, Ralph Hodge, was a former executive at ICI before joining our board. He was very good friends with the chief executive at the time. If we didn't close the deal by a certain hour, he was going to call the CEO and then have that CEO call the deal guy and tell him to stop immediately and sign the deal. The hour was approaching and my heart was pounding. A very frustrated part of me wanted the call to come in just to teach him a lesson. Seconds before the deadline, the deal was signed and I called Ralph and canceled the call. On the day of closure for ICI, March 29, we filed suit in Houston court on J-Block, received a summons by Phillips and waited on a commissioning date notice on the lawsuit. There was no time to celebrate even for the evening. It was an amazing series of events. Frankly, I don't know how we survived it.

April and May were marked by the filing of four additional lawsuits, for a grand total of six. All this because Phillips wouldn't sign a deal that was great for them and one that would set the pace in the North Sea. In fact, our proposal would have provided the J-Block partners more than $1,000,000,000 in revenue between our cash payment, natural gas flows and crude flows of 100,000 bbls/day and all of that was in the first year. That fact just added to everyone's frustration. It also fueled everyone's passion to get nasty and turn up the "low road" tactics. We discussed many strategies that the team developed, including possible negotiation solutions and possible negative situations to add leverage if Phillips were simply going to fight us to the death just because they could. Their president had the ultimate comment at the time. He stated, "We are more interested in principal then NPV." I wonder what their shareholders thought of that little statement.

2

MORE LAWSUITS

Each week was filled with new adventure in litigation and contract positioning. Things spiraled downhill from a commercial perspective very quickly. One good thing came out of the difficult QBR: Bob Williams, the manager of litigation for ECT, came over to help us. Bob and I became very close friends, and he remains someone I respect greatly today. Robin Gibbs, a world-class litigator, also joined our team. We eventually hired four top law firms, including the mighty Joe Jamail. If we could keep a suit in Houston, our case would be strong and I was sure we could win. The legal experts' input over the next two months was invaluable and helped the English litigation team greatly. The English team was a daily disaster, especially when compared to Gibbs. The entire process was ugly. Of course, the English lawyers did not appreciate the American invasion or any attempts to help.

In early May, we even lost a lawsuit that we had considered a sure thing, the first round of the commissioning date hearing. Their Queens Counsel (QC, the highest ranking of senior barristers) simply beat us, which made everyone nervous about the future of the English litigation activities and cast some doubt on our team's work and ability to assess the situation. We soon felt even sicker when our original QC, one of the top in the country, a very senior fellow named Anthony Grabiner, suddenly dismissed himself from the case due to a conflict of interest with Amoco. He didn't use a computer and learned of the conflict at the last minute. Amoco undoubtedly planned this and we were not granted any additional time so we scrambled for a new QC. It made us aware of just how nasty this was going to be. Amoco had totally finessed us. Anthony was also very confident and actually gave us a 100 percent chance of winning. I had never heard that before but it was all over a legal concept called "an agreement to agree" that was unenforceable in English law. We had 300 years of precedent on our side. This challenged my credibility.

The doubt grew even worse when we lost the anti-suit injunction in June. The injunction was to stop the other lawsuit. It wasn't the fact that we lost, but the manner in which we lost that caused the problem. The judge was against us from the very beginning. He actually made fun of the American judicial system and the U.S. Constitution. The events sickened us, and Mary Nell almost stopped the proceedings to ask for an apology. This ugly trend continued. We were granted an expedited appeal and thought our luck had finally changed, but we lost the expedited appeal almost as soon as we had been granted it. If ever anything deserved an expedited status, this did. Our concern for the impending, remaining litigation grew.

In May, I received an offer to move back to Houston in December of 1996. It was surprising and caused a lot of difficult decisions and discussions about our future. Chris and I cried and worried a lot about our future and what was best for the family and the design of our lifestyles for the future. Many changed occurred over the summer, and they added to the difficulty of the decision. Mark Frevert and Dan McCarty decided to move to London. I knew Mark and Dan very well. Mark was my boss twice at Enron and Dan was my attorney in my first job at the pipeline. We made quite a team and had fun together. That threw the politics of the move home into a mystery. My boss and friend, Geoff Roberts, also had a difficult decision to make and announced that he would be going back in September, versus December, without having a definite position. In late July, Chris and I went back to Houston to look for a house without knowing what job I would have or how much we should spend on it. Would the next job be great or one that wasn't satisfying? Chris started the job of house hunting and quickly learned that she liked a "grand" house, which didn't fit well with the idea of being conservative. A conversation with Jeff Skilling topped off the whole episode. He called me into his office and told me that he really needed me to stay in London and keep working on J-Block. At this point, I had not had a great deal of discussion with Jeff on the J-Block issue. This was a "Corp" problem, not an ECT problem. He was very persuasive and I had to go home and tell Chris that it was off and we were staying. This time in our lives was an emotional rollercoaster.

October 11, 1996 is a day I will never forget. Our luck was about to change. The Court of Appeals reversed our commissioning date loss (our sure thing) and saved us $175 million. And, the decision came in the day before a big scheduled meeting between Rich Kinder and Jim Mulva. I was on cloud nine; we felt vindicated for a great deal of work by our entire team. However, my credibility was still on the line. At 2:30 p.m., we called everyone in the company together and made the announcement. Richard Harper came up with the original idea of our position on the commissioning date. This was his value, enormous value. He would receive the largest bonus of his life and boy, was it deserved. It was fun and a very proud moment to me personally.

The next trial, on the validity of the start date, finally began on October 28 and was immediately recessed for two weeks. The judge wanted time to read the opening statements (only in Britain). Finally, on November 11, it began again, for real. The trial opened with a bang and we struck some heavy body blows against the CATS parties. It would be foreshadowing of things to come. Over the next three months, the trial would go as well as it could go for us. We still had some difficult days; however, the other side took a constant pounding. It was very difficult so sit through those days in court, and soon I found myself going only occasionally. The QCs did a very good job and outclassed the other side. It is scary to think that we truly believed our odds would improve so dramatically with better representation by our QCs. Our people simply outplayed the opposition, but the overall frustration with the English legal system never ended.

The negotiation discussions continued at a very slow pace during the trial. Disturbingly slow. Finally, in December, the discussion came back once again. The J-Block partners sent us a long proposal. It was terrible and actually more of a wish list, but when you broke it down there was something we could work with. The negotiations were heavy and we sent a counter (with real detail) on December 20. For the second Christmas in a row, I wondered if I would return home with the family for a real holiday. I didn't actually know until we got on the plane. The other side waited until after the holiday to get back to us and begin the next and intense leg of the deal.

January started with a bang, and the negotiations were finally ending. It appeared that 1997 would be the year. The deal included a cash payment of $350 million; a 100 mmcf/d take or pay commitment; tiered gas pricing and for the first time we committed to withdrawal our article 85 submittal to the European Union. BG must have been in the loop fully on this negotiation. The proposal was very strong and provided the J-Block partners more than $900 million of total cash flow in 1997 alone. At least we thought it would. For weeks, we worked to move toward closure with a deadline of February 1. For the first time, everyone was at the table and working hard to complete the deal. Mind you, they were not being reasonable, but we were able to find ways around all the obstacles they put in front of us. The cash price was $350 million up front. What a huge figure! But, even with that and the other terms that we put in, we still were saving $500 million for Enron (half a billion dollars!). The pressure was on, and we handled it. I was so proud of the team. Finally, on Friday, January 23, we sent our final offer and proposal to the parties. On Saturday, we received a phone call from Jim Mulva at Phillips that killed the deal without even a counter offer, even though we had worked out almost everything. It was outrageous; he stated that we were still $200 million apart. The deal died, and we all took a much-needed breather.

It actually got worse a couple of weeks later. Ken was involved and called Wayne Allen directly. They had a meeting in mid January. Our expectations were high because Wayne was Jim Mulva's boss and that deal died strangely and inappropriately. We thought that maybe Ken and Wayne could get it back on track. We had very big expectations. We were to be disappointed. Wayne told Ken that we were even farther apart then Jim had even indicated! Another $60 million. He even explained why the $350 million cash wasn't that great due to their tax position. They discounted it by $110 million. They didn't offer an alternative for the value however. It made no sense if they wanted to find a solution. The next day, I drafted a letter for Ken to send to him to officially close the door on any further talks and restate our position and confusion. It still felt like a tactic but one that didn't make a lot of sense.

It started out as a typical morning, but that would soon change. I was on my way to work on the Number 17 double-decker bus when it hit me. It was time to make the big cash offer to the J-Block partners and offer them a daily take or pay obligation. Just eliminate any make-up rights and take the entire "trust" factor away. Trust would no longer be an issue: If we didn't take the gas, we paid anyway. I thought Jeff would be receptive because it was still new in his administration and he could eat the big company hit. I ran to the office and got on the phone. Even the J-Block partners couldn't turn this down and it was the right time for the company to take the hit. Rich was never prepared to do that and get this problem off the table, but this was the right thing to do and the right time to do it. Jeff agreed with the strategy and it was time to make the final push to end the war.

A few weeks after the collapse of the deal, we let it leak out that I was returning to Houston and that we were giving up and turning it all over to the lawyers to fight to the death. I wasn't sure there was anything else to do. It seemed we needed to make a change and maybe someone else could be the catalyst to get it done. But, in April, the negotiations came back again. It seemed never to stop. It was a very difficult time for my family. This time Jeff Skilling led the negotiations, doing an excellent job of not only negotiating but also managing Jim Mulva. Everyone on both sides worked very hard and appeared to make real progress. For the first week of the negotiations, I couldn't tell anyone what I was doing (per Mulva's instructions). The group and I worked like dogs to move things along and meet deadlines. We made all of ours but they, of course, did not. The pace and number of different activities was amazing.

RESOLUTION

On April 18, we proposed a new deal consisting of $400 million in cash 85 percent daily take or pay and gave the partners a great deal of flexibility to deliver gas to us. The total volume obligation went from 834 bcf to 900 bcf. It was quite a move. By mid-April, we were able to include other people and put a final deal on the table on May 1. It appeared the stars were aligned this time for getting something closed. The terms included a cash payment of $440 million; the price went to 64 percent of contract price for all gas taken; daily take or pay—no make up rights, which took all trust out of the deal. We paid for all the gas even if we didn't take it and it was on a monthly basis. There was no wriggle room thus, they could know that no matter what, their gas would flow. It also settled the CATS dispute and all the litigations. The pending decision was the deadline we were using to get the deal done. It also set base contract to 834-bcf total. We took out all put options and reserve risk and made everything very clear. We also had to withdrawal the EU submission as expected. This is one thing that I believe BG brought to the table. Although they probably believed our submission would not have been successful, they were risking everything on that bet with a very uncontrollable entity.

At one point the expected happened, Phillips turned it down, and we knew it had to be a ploy. We had given them what they wanted, and the value items that they complained about were even confirmed by the Phillips' CFO as acceptable. The deal all but died once again. Jeff did a great job of keeping it alive, and then Jim brought it back to the table as we had expected him to do. It was quite a bold move, letting it die, but we knew it was the only way ever to close the deal. On May 21, the big guys started talking again and verbally closed the deal. Then the fun started. The final negotiations began and started very slowly, especially considering that the deal had been done. We spent the next few days waiting for Phillips to get their work together. It was unbelievably stressful. I had many conversations with Phillips' Associate General Counsel Clyde Lea, and we had to trust each other under strange and very surreal circumstances. My gut said to trust him but also to manage the situation. All of the negotiations were happening in London.

Toward the end, I made a call that had political suicide written all over it. I asked Jeff Skilling to come to London and be on the ground in case I needed him in the negotiation. I had planned to bring him out as a surprise if the J-Block parties attempted to change the deal, which I knew he would. Even thinking about this today puts a pit in my stomach. There was a very good chance that he would not be needed at all, and that and he would sit in his hotel room and "waste" his time completely. Jeff really didn't like to travel overseas, and he had the busiest schedule of probably anyone in the country. After a couple of days of waiting and holding our position, the local executives called a meeting, at the end of which it was my view that the deal was not going to happen under the agreed timeframe. I believed they were stalling for time and exit strategies; something wasn't right. I blew up and shut the deal down. It was late one night and I felt I had to make the call. It was the gutsiest thing I had ever done. But, I had to change what was going on. I felt that if we didn't, the deal would never actually close. I felt I was putting my career on the line though because we had never gotten this far before. I knew I was right, though. Jeff and Ken supported me completely and showed just how much faith they had in our team. Jim Mulva then called Jeff Skilling and Skilling agreed to come to London and join in the process (they didn't know he had already planned to be there!). It worked beautifully, but it was not without personal risk. We had to have this deal and it was mine to lose at this point. Jim Mulva kept his word, although the process was ugly.

It is strange to write about it after the fact, because it seems like a dream—or a nightmare, really. Everyone on the team had worked themselves to exhaustion. At one point I had about 11 hours of real sleep over the course of five days, and I felt that my body was about to give out. On the final day, I actually fell asleep, or passed out, and discovered later that I slept in a pile of broken glass on the floor. I didn't care. I closed my eyes at about 3 a.m., and at 4 a.m., two tax guys awakened me, talking about a huge issue that they had discovered. The head of tax, Jordan Mintz (the absolute best taxman in the business) was discussing what to do. I began waking up thinking, why is there such a heated discussion about tax this late in the game? I thought in a sleepy state with my eyes still closed, "Tax problem, a tax problem? Bad." I woke up with a rush of adrenaline. We solved the problem; as usual, they found a solution, and we moved on. I was so exhausted but was astonished to watch Mary Nell lead her effort with a lot more stamina. I still don't know how she did it. She was a 100-pound fighting force.

I have many memories of the negotiations, including frequent trips with the group (including Skilling) to McDonalds across the street and watching our highly respected president being very normal and bringing in Egg McMuffins for everyone. The last few days were full of secret meetings with Agip, which included secret calls from outside the partner meetings, secret strategy sessions with Clyde, thoughts of killing everyone on the other side, laughing at Clyde's expressions: "We're going to get there, dealing with my partners are like herding cats" and wondering why we do such things for a living.

Everyone on the team did a fantastic job. If one single person failed at his or her assignment in any way, we would not have been able to get this deal done. Lord knows that the J-Block side and Freshfields, their lawyers, would not have known how to make it happen. Upon Jim Mulva's physical arrival, the negotiations broke into five parallel discussions, and I had to bring in many extra people to do the deal. At one point, Enron had 23 people actually up at Freshfields' office doing a piece of the transaction. There was something very funny about my role: I didn't enter a single deal session. I supervised the entire process and kept it on track. My job was like the old vaudeville act of the man that spun dishes on sticks. It was all timing and execution. There was one time I was actually sitting there at 1 a.m. with nothing to do. I actually called Mom and Dad during one such occasion. It was very interesting being the boss and executive. I was able to make it all happen, and I learned once again that it takes a special talent to pull off something like this. It was great for my personal development and self-confidence. I sure don't think of myself as anything special but we did pull it off. It was a beautiful thing, watching Mary Nell and Richard in other rooms performing magnificently.

On June 2 at 12 p.m., we signed the agreements. It took two hours to execute the 64 agreements, with about 50 people watching. As we got ready to sign, the lawyers announced that due to the materiality of the event, once we started signing, no one could leave the room. We all went to the bathroom and the impact of just how big this was hit us all again. I signed for Enron Corp., Enron Europe and TGTL. By a strange, small oversight, Jeff couldn't sign as an attorney-in-fact the way the documents were written and so couldn't sign for Enron. The president was left out of the entire signing event! I think he found it somewhat funny. He couldn't be too mad, with everyone killing himself or herself to get this done, and he knew it. While signing I remember looking at Jeff across the table. He just smiled a knowing smile. I had tears in my eyes because we were actually doing it; everyone had worked so hard and had given total and complete commitment. Jeff's smile told me he was happy for me and for all the work that we had done to make this happen. It was one of the proudest moments in my life. The feeling was very strange. I was actually numb. I wanted to scream with joy and cry but I had to maintain my composure. After all, as far as the producers know, they had taken us to cleaners. After it we had finished, I was in shock and disbelief. I hugged Skilling and Harper. We gave out deal pens, about 30 of them, and at the end of the signing; everyone shook hands and smiled, as we waited for the confirmation of the money transfer. Sending $440 million is actually quite difficult. Upon confirmation, we whisked off to analyst and media calls and watched the stock. We ended up issuing releases and confirming the deal before we actually confirmed the money. This was a wild set of decision-making with the minutes counting down before the opening of the stock exchange in New York. It had a funny twist to it because BG didn't have a very senior person around to make the decision. The most senior person available wasn't even a corporate officer and I thought he was going to have a heart attack making the call with all these senior executives doing so for their companies. Everyone had their press releases on the fax machines ready to go at the same time. What an odd event. This would be a good deal for all the companies.

A MATTER OF PRINCIPLES

Many people within Enron wondered if this was a good deal. My memory of Skilling dancing to the background music while waiting for the analyst call says it all. Everyone was worried about the stock market but the stock didn't really move; it ended down 3/4 of a point but ironically not due to J-Block. The $675 million write off ($1.80 per share) was because we had announced we were short of our second quarter earnings target by a few cents due to a domestic natural gas liquids issue. What a fickle market. I actually passed out on the analyst call. I fell asleep in a taxi on the way home. When I got home, Chris put me right into a bath (boy did I need it). She told me later that I looked like I a prisoner of war. I had lost several pounds that week which I couldn't afford as a very thin person. It was also very hard on me due to my diabetes. We weren't eating well, or at all, and stress is the number one influence on moving blood counts. My fingers were bloody from all of the blood checks that I had made, especially those last few days. I actually fell asleep in the bath. Chris she put me in bed and I woke up 14 hours later. I have no memories at all of the events once I passed out. Our lives had returned. This lifted the weight of the world from my shoulders. Nothing I write can properly articulate the events of the day.

That next morning was full of relaxing. Chris and I had breakfast outside in bathrobes in the bright sunshine. But, work showed up again soon. I got a call informing me that we had lost the CATS trial. Not only had we lost, we were killed. The judge destroyed us and I was on the phone working on press releases immediately. No rest for the weary. I survived and, frankly, nothing could upset me much on that day. We had taken the worst case in consideration of the write down so it had no financial impact. We may have lost the lawsuit but we had settled the biggest issue, the J-Block piece.

That same day, the press started coming out with all the stories. That was quite an experience. Reading about your own deal in the media was very strange. I felt a little like a director in a play reading everyone's critiques of our performance. The press was especially harsh in the UK but much more favorable in the US. I kept many of the articles for my scrapbook, especially from the *Houston Chronicle*, *Wall Street Journal* and the *London Times*. The deal made the front page of the business section and it would look good framed.

In the end, it was my relationship and trust with Ernesto Sarpi that really got the deal done. He was a great person and truly wanted to find a solution and put this behind them all. He and his company Agip were able to take the emotion out of the deal and get to a solution. I am sure the partnership would have been very upset if they knew of all our meetings and discussions, but we both had the right intent and found the way to put this problem behind us all. Without question, there would have been no deal without him.

To this day, I have great respect for Ernie, and I treasure a gift he presented me at our farewell and celebration dinner. We went to dinner and had a very expensive meal with expensive wine. At the dinner, he presented us with a picture from his wife's family that they had carried around with them for their entire marriage. His generosity moved me and made me feel embarrassed, because I didn't bring a special gift for them. In many ways, the Europeans have the right idea over Americans.

Each of the principles I discussed in the preceding business chapters section of this book is applicable to my involvement with the J-Block deal. I tried to lay them out in such a way that will make it easy for you to trace back to the story above.

Conclusions

I have said a lot in this book. I have never pretended to be a talented author; rather I am simply a blessed person who wanted to share some lessons learned. I'm just a kid from Oklahoma who cared and worked hard. I guess you could say that I made a lot out of the gifts that God has bestowed on me.

This book was an exploration. An exploration of self, an attempt to define my life and how I became the man I am today. I have attempted to lay out some of the principles that led to my success and happiness. You can never hit everything, but I had to try to write my story. If I hadn't, then so much of what I have said or believed would have just gone away with me. I hope that this flawed man is now at least trying to walk the talk and make the world a slightly better place by sharing some thoughts and activities. Better said, I am trying to share some things that I have learned so that others won't make the same mistakes I made along the way.

Someone asked me recently about what I look for in considering a new job or position. The answer is simple. If I am asked to boil it down to just one sentence, I would answer that question with the statement, "I want to be an impact player." Some on the surface might think that is to have power or recognition or simply to be greedy. It is not. It is to have an impact in many phases of life, not just the business. The success of the business is a result of having an impact on helping people to live up to their potential. It is simply the matter of cause and effect. If your only goal is to close a deal or make money, you probably won't attain it or, if you do, it will be a great deal harder or more costly. Maybe in ways that you didn't see coming. Is it really worth it to be rich or powerful and be divorced with your kids dealing with you not being around or never seeing you on the weekends?

I hope my book will help you. Writing this book was scary because I put myself into it and really exposed my feelings and beliefs. It's not an easy thing to share your inner self with the world. The goal was not to have you follow my words to the letter but for you to pick out items that make sense and make you think. Even if you totally disagree with a topic or philosophy, think about it. I am convinced it had an effect on me, so I hope you will not dismiss anything out of hand. If you disagree, disagree, but please don't dismiss.

This book is about action. Take an action step. Here are a few action items that I can say had a high impact on me. This is my top 20.

- Keep a journal or write down your thoughts and feelings.
- When you get inspired or have an idea, write it down.
- Do your brainstorming list on what you are grateful for and review it often.
- Look at affirmations.
- Always learn. Improve yourself in some way. What a great investment with huge returns.
- Read inspiring books. You can't help but identify with something and realize what you can truly achieve when you set your mind to it. They changed a life or the world; you should think about that.
- Allow yourself to be inspired or moved. Put yourself in a position to be amazed.
- Try asking yourself empowering questions. Make your list of three questions and see what happens.
- Watch *It's a Wonderful Life* often.
- Live with passion in everything you do.
- Surround yourself with positive people.
- Your integrity is everything; don't ever compromise it.
- Take responsibility and accountability for your actions.
- Set goals and objectives in your personal and business life.
- Model yourself after someone you respect or from whom you want to learn. Make the call and talk to him or her.
- Take action. Just do it.
- Go to church; read the Bible; pray. Pray often.
- Make a list of your code of conduct. What are your principals that you won't compromise?
- Laugh a lot; don't take yourself so seriously.
- Think about the balance in your life. Do you need a re-alignment?
- Remember, the harder you work, the more luck you have.

In attempting to find answers about myself and the driving forces behind the results of life, one thing is clear. There is no one thing, one person, one job that is responsible for it. It is the combination of all areas of your life. You must have the right fabric, however. The text is broken into three sections, but all areas are woven together. Which drove which area the most? That I don't know but examining all areas of my life is my attempt to figure it out. You can do the same with your life.

The final product of this book is significantly different from what I had at the beginning, and it pained me to change it. Legal issues drove me to take out my collection of affirmations and drop some direct, applicable parts of the book written by others. It pained me to edit all of that out but our choices were limited. When I am referencing a book, I can't suggest more strongly just going to your neighborhood bookstore and picking up the book I was referencing. You can read more about an area I was discussing or simply keep it around and maybe someday later and pick it up at a future date.

I am so very grateful that you would take time in your life to read this book. I am very humbled by your time commitment and your choice to give me a chance to have a conversation with you and to share with you the lessons about one man's journey. Good luck in your journey. I hope you have a great and peaceful life.

APPENDIX A

What am I thankful for?

Live with an attitude of gratitude

1. My wife
2. My children
3. My children's health
4. The love of my children
5. Jesus
6. My health
7. Liking my wife
8. Having good kids
9. My standard of living
10. Living in America
11. My education
12. My family all being alive and well
13. Not having regrets in life
14. My attitude
15. Being an optimist
16. Clarity on life and business issues
17. Knowing what is right from wrong
18. My relationship with God
19. Being thin

20. Not having complications from diabetes

21. Not dying or having side effects

22. Being attractive

23. My personality

24. My parents

25. Not doing bad things

26. Being excited about silly things

27. Being funny

28. Being liked

29. My blue eyes

30. Seeing and traveling to great places

31. Having a lot of money

32. Having my children's college paid for

33. My car

34. My friends

35. My possessions

36. My job

37. Being appreciated at work

38. Having a good church

39. My daily life

40. Not worrying about money or the future

41. Not going bald

42. Not having bladder cancer

43. Having movies flow through me

44. Being silly

45. Drinking coffee, watching an old movie and reading the paper on weekend mornings

46. My clothes

47. My art collection

48. My art passion

49. My time at Enron

50. My ability to relate to people

51. Enjoying music the way I do

52. Being inspirable

53. Discovering books on tape

54. Having the ability to help people

55. Feeling good about my life's path

56. Abbie

57. Exercising stock options over the years

58. Living conservatively

59. Being honest

60. Going to England and working on J-block

61. My membership at Champions

62. My love of golf

63. Being a decent golfer

64. Having excellent business vision

65. My friends

66. My travels

67. Keeping a journal and understanding perspective

68. Keeping affirmations

69. Going to OU

70. Joining Sig Ep in 1978

71. Sooner football

Appendix B

Personal Goals and Objectives

Goals
Updated: July 2000

"A goal not written is only a wish"

<u>**Family**</u>
to be a great dad

- to raise good kids

  - read books

  - talk to Chris

  - discuss with other parents

  - review Claire's work

  - review reference material

  - more time at home

  - tell and show you like them

- to have fun with the kids

  - plan special activities

  - Claire dates

  - more active on sports activities

  - Saturday sports

  - plan special activities for each child

- Indian princess
- Indian guides
- Father/child activities
- Claire: Sunday events, morning TV
- Michael: play, rough house
- more focus on bedtime
- more involvement with their activities
- be here now
- to prepare our kids for life
  - talks and teachable moments
  - lead by example
  - give them the gift of optimism
- to be patient
  - take a step back and don't react at the time
  - remember they are children

to be a good provider

- to provide for college expenses
- 4 year private university
- MBA
- to provide a trust fund to give them long term security
- pay for help to allow Chris and me to free up time
- housekeeper
- lawn
- handyman
- pool man

to give the children the gift of optimism

- talk to them about unlimited possibilities
- the gift of appreciation

to be wealthy and independent

- to accomplish financial goals
  - Misner—financial advisor
  - asset allocation
  - tax help
  - estate planning
  - maintain will

to have good health

- diabetes
- monitor carefully
- sleep
  - go to bed earlier
- generally take care of my body
  - exercise—buy home equipment
  - force some activity and add to schedule
  - to have a happy marriage

to be a great husband

- be nicer to Chris
- be more supportive
- initiate more help around the house
- less focus on the physical

- hug more

- massage and rub more

- spend more time at home

to have balance

- continually review goals and life

- difficulty and conflicts

to be confident and relaxed at home

- sleep well

- control thoughts and relax and let go

- be here now

PERSONAL
to be a good golfer

- have a handicap of 10

- access to a club and range

- spend time playing and practicing

- introduce Claire and Michael to the game

- get Chris to play

- go to driving range more often

to travel at will

- take 1 big trip per year with Chris alone

- to see exotic places

- take Chris on business trips

- to stay in the nice places and resorts

- to have the ability to travel with the family
- take 1 big trip a year with kids
- memories for kids as foundation
- smaller day versions

to help others with diabetes

- to be a role model
- talk openly about it
- help others
- join Diabetes association
- to become active in association
- help at Enron
- join JDF board

to be a positive influence on people

- lead by example
- share viewpoints and affirmations
- be the most positive person in a group
- read affirmations and inspirational articles

to be asked for advice

- be an approachable person
- keep confidences
- be willing to help

to be an impact player in life and work

- work on important things

- always move forward

to be nice to people

- focus on giving vs. receiving

- give back to community

- give to church

to do more volunteer work

- with Chris

- work with kids

- church

- diabetes

- arthritis

to be less self-centered

- do nice things for people

- give time and $ to others

- be nicer to people, see above

to get into politics

- to be a member of a board

- charity or work

- to join the school board

- get active in Claire's school

- PTA

- attend meetings

- to be President of the US

- be active in Republican party

- participate in political events

- use work for contacts

- do above and see if Chris is comfortable

to be an outstanding dresser

- keep up wardrobe

- have own style

to add my signature to help people

- touch peoples lives

- take the time

- see all above

Work
to enjoy work

- to have a good boss

- run a business unit or division

- light but good travel

- impact player

to be looked at as a leader of people

- lead by example

- bring out the best in people

- empowerment and feedback

- act as a coach versus a supervisor

- try different things

to be well rounded

- finance exposure
- English refresher
- attend offered courses
- take 1 major course every year
- exposure to new things

to be a good speaker

- take advantage of all opportunities for practice
- toastmasters

to help people

- be a supportive boss
- look for ways to assist people
- PRC

to rub elbows with important people and learn from them

- to be in the right position and job
- take advantage of opportunities when they arise

to be in the inner loop

- to have people's trust
- keep people's trust

to be in the right position or area within Enron

- focus on future activities
- make a difference
- talk to people and get their views

- take advantage of opportunities
- add value

to make big bonuses

- positioning
- ranking
- balance problems and conflicts

to be a balanced worker

- difficulty with other goals
- combination of all above

<u>Spiritual</u>
to be a good Christian

- make it a priority
- live in a Christian way
- think about God
- read bible
- watch religious movies and programs
- read inspirational books
- pray often

to raise good Christian children

- pray at meals
- discuss God openly
- read the bible and religious stories

to be a regular and good member of church

- attend church every week

- give financial support

- become active member

- join bible study

- take classes

- join a committee

- teach children

- vestry or executive committee

Material
to drive a nice car

- BMW/Mercedes

- Grand Cherokee

to live in a magnificent home

- big lot in a nice area

- Huntwick Estates

- see house listing

- get proper help

- architect

- builder

- decorator

to be a member of a golf club

- Champions

to have an outstanding art collection

- buy additional interesting work at auction

- have 1 piece from all 20th century masters

- bring pieces back from Europe

- old maps

- old prints

- move into oils

- Christies

- local

- sculptures

- rugs and tapestries

- stained glass window from a church

- British telephone booth

to learn to paint

- take art classes back in Houston

- set up area in house for painting

- sculpting/print making

to learn to act

- take a class

- join in on a local playhouse

to learn to write creatively

- take a class

- keep a journal as practice

- write a story or piece

APPENDIX C

List of my favorite impact books

Read inspirational authors

Norman Vincent Peale

- *The Power of Positive Thinking*

Anthony Robbins

- *Unlimited Power*

- *Personal Power*

Denis Waitley

- *The Psychology of Winning*

- *Timing is Everything*

Og Mandino

- *The Choice*

- *Mission Success*

- *The Greatest Miracle in the World*

Spencer Johnson

- *Who Moved My Cheese*

- *The Present*

Rick Warren

- *The Purpose Driven Life*

Jim Collins

- *Good to Great*

The Bible

Read books, watch movies that stretch your imagination

- Biographies of successful people
- Books on the history of the presidency
- The history of the universe
- Science fiction
- Try all kinds and a variety
- Books in your field
- Learn all the time

Watch religious and inspirational movies

- *The Ten Commandments*
- *Field of Dreams*
- *Sergeant York*
- *The Greatest Story Ever Told*
- *Superman*
- *Indiana Jones and the Temple of Doom*
- *Indiana Jones and the Last Crusade*
- *Rocky*
- *Joshua*

APPENDIX D

A few great lists of how to be successful

Success secrets from a great coach:

- Fear no opponent. Respect every opponent.
- Remember, it's the perfection of the smallest details that makes big things happen.
- Keep in mind that hustle makes up for many a mistake.
- Be more interested in character than reputation.
- Be quick, but don't hurry.
- Understand that the harder you work the more luck you will have.
- Know that valid self-analysis is crucial for improvement.
- Remember that there is no substitute for hard work and careful planning. Failing to prepare is preparing to fail.

10 Rules for success:

1. Find your particular talent.
2. Be big.
3. Be honest.
4. Live with enthusiasm.
5. Don't let you possessions possess you.
6. Don't worry about problems.
7. Look up to people when you can; down to no one.

8. Don't cling to the past.

9. Assume your full share of responsibility in the world.

10. Pray consistently and confidently.

Four-mula for success:

1. Show up on time.

2. Do what you say you will do.

3. Finish what you start.

4. Say please and thank you.

Four-mula for success:

1. Choose a career you love.

2. Give it the best there is in you.

3. Seize your opportunities.

4. Be a member of the team.

APPENDIX E

My Keys to Success

Keys to Success

Integrity; it is not just a word, it's a way of life
Be reliable, diligent and honest
Have an understating with your boss
Set goals and objectives
Model yourself after the best
Make a difference; have real accomplishments
Be a player at your company or area
Take risks in your career
Focus on what is best for the company or the customer; not on how to make money for yourself
You can always vote with your feet

Successful Management attributes

Lead by example
Promote teamwork
Empower your employees
Recognize good work and extra effort
Show your work ethic
Focus on communication
Create goals and objectives

Lessons Learned

Don't stray from you principles; ever
Believe in yourself
Don't do something stupid
When you do, learn from it

Do what is asked for and then over-deliver
Continue to learn especially in areas that you have a weakness
Share credit every time
Don't look back
Outwork the competition
Treat people with respect, at all levels
Build a support system
Don't be afraid to ask for help or advice
When in command, take command
Do thorough performance reviews
Do a self evaluation performance review
Work like an Olympian
Dress the part
Look at failure as feedback
Change is inevitable, be ready and welcome it
Remember, not making a decision is a decision
Live with passion

APPENDIX F

Life Timeline

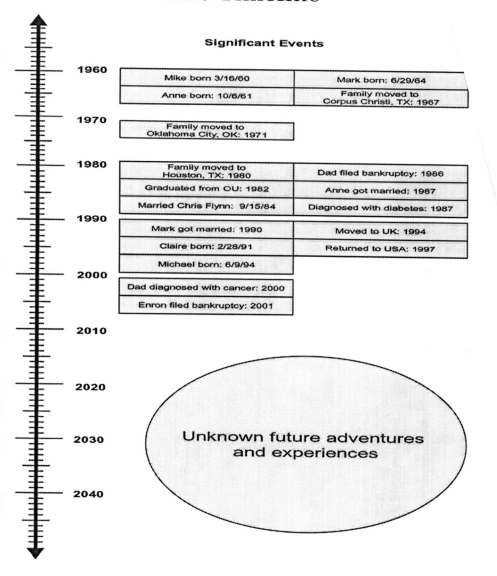

Significant Events

1960

| Mike born 3/16/60 | Mark born: 6/29/64 |
| Anne born: 10/6/61 | Family moved to Corpus Christi, TX: 1967 |

1970

Family moved to Oklahoma City, OK: 1971

1980

Family moved to Houston, TX: 1980	Dad filed bankruptcy: 1986
Graduated from OU: 1982	Anne got married: 1987
Married Chris Flynn: 9/15/84	Diagnosed with diabetes: 1987

1990

Mark got married: 1990	Moved to UK: 1994
Claire born: 2/28/91	Returned to USA: 1997
Michael born: 6/9/94	

2000

Dad diagnosed with cancer: 2000

Enron filed bankruptcy: 2001

2010

2020

2030

Unknown future adventures and experiences

2040

Life Timeline

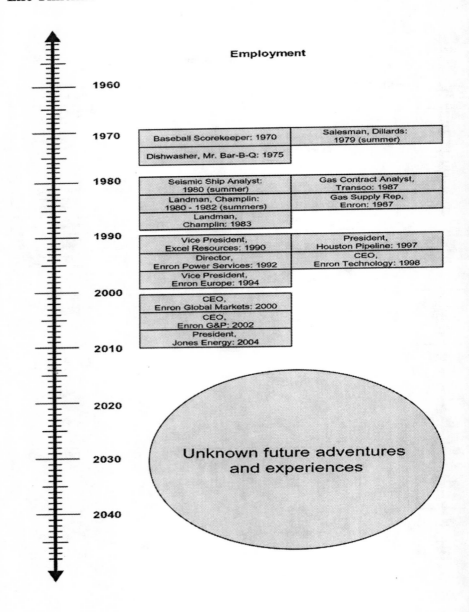

Your Life Timeline

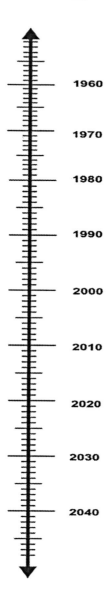

About the Author

Mike S. McConnell

Mike is currently President of Jones Energy, Ltd., an oil and gas exploration company headquartered in Austin, Texas. His responsibilities and focus includes the company P&L and all various commercial activities.

After leaving Enron, he formed and became President of McConnell Management, LLC. His spectrum of activities included consulting services for several companies inside and outside the energy industry.

In February 2002, Mike McConnell returned to Enron to become the Chairman and Chief Executive Officer for the Generation and Production Group. He was responsible for the unregulated businesses for the emerging post Chapter 11 Company. He led and developed the business plan for the Generation and Production Group, which initially consisted of thirty-three unregulated individual natural gas and power assets in North, Central and South America. His day-to-day responsibilities included the operations and P&L for the North American unregulated businesses until the plan of reorganization received court approval. Ultimately, the plan of reorganization was redesigned to include only three regulated pipelines with all unregulated businesses moved into the liquidation group. Prior to completing his duties on April 30, 2003, Mike was a member of the Enron Executive Committee and reported directly to the Office of the Chief Executive.

Mike was Chairman and Chief Executive Officer for Enron Global Markets until the bankruptcy filing in December 2001. He assumed this position in August 2000. His responsibilities included running the business unit, which included the following global trading and origination businesses for Enron: Crude & Products, Coal, Emissions, Shipping, LNG, Weather, Freight, the Financial Trading groups and Insurance Risk Management. He was also responsible for Enron Japan. Mike was a member of Enron's Management Committee.

Previously, Mike was Vice Chairman and Chief Operating Officer for Enron Net Works, which was the business unit that combined Enron's global technology and market-making capabilities to create electronic businesses and market places. Before moving to Enron Net Works, Mike was the Chief Executive

Officer—Global Technology. His areas of responsibility included all of Information Technology and eCommerce for Enron Corp. Prior to Global Technology, Mike was President of Houston Pipe Line Company (HPL) and Louisiana Resources Company (LRC) where he was responsible for all of the unregulated natural gas and transmission assets in North America. Prior to being appointed President of Houston Pipe Line Company, Mike was a Vice President for Enron Europe in the London office.

In addition, Mike has also held positions in the Enron Power Services, Gas Supply and Marketing areas of Enron. He has worked in the energy industry for over 20 years including positions as a landman, various gas supply and marketing positions as well as being the Vice President and a Principal for an independent natural gas company.

Mike graduated from the University of Oklahoma in 1982 with a BBA in Petroleum Land Management with an emphasis on Law. He is currently serving on the Board of Advisors for the Price College of Business at the University of Oklahoma. Mike has previously held positions as a member of the Board of Directors for Mariner Energy Company, Inc., Bridgeline Holdings, Inc., Citrus Trading Corp, the Houston Energy Association, the Texas Intrastate Pipeline Association, Enron Europe, Teesside Gas Transportation Limited (TGTL—a joint venture between Enron and ICI), Juvenile Diabetes Research Foundation and the Vestry of St. Dustan's Episcopal Church. Mike has a wife and two children. He is also active in his church and enjoys collecting art and playing golf.

Please e-mail Mike at *mike_s_mcconnell@hotmail.com* if you would like additional information or wish to share your feedback.

978-0-595-42851-
0-595-42851-7

Printed in the United States
96249LV00004B/117/A